Contents

In association with

bournemouth
symphony orchestra

BSOlive.com

1

Foreword

I have had the great privilege of being the Chief Conductor of the Bournemouth Symphony Orchestra since 2008 and it has been a fantastic journey.

We have toured, enjoyed great BBC Proms success, played opera in concert, completed our groundbreaking recordings of Prokofiev, performed spectacular outdoor events and delighted and challenged our audiences with a huge range of pieces, some very familiar, others not so well known.

This is just some of what we have achieved together and it is one of the reasons I extended my contract with the BSO back in 2013.

The other is my relationship with the musicians. From the very first time we played together, it has always been incredibly special. They are always an inspiration.

The BSO has been described as "one of this country's cultural miracles" and I wholeheartedly endorse that.

It has a global reputation.

We are already planning our concerts for 2018, a year that will also see the small matter of the BSO's 125th anniversary, an incredible milestone which we are all looking forward to immensely.

It has been an honour to follow in the footsteps of distinguished conductors such as Sir Dan Godfrey, Sir Charles Groves, Constantin Silvestri, Paavo Berglund and Andrew Litton, to name but five.

I am very conscious of the history and tradition of the Bournemouth Symphony Orchestra and I know how much the BSO means to its supporters and to Bournemouth, Poole and beyond.

It has been a great adventure so far. I am so proud of what we have achieved and I know there is plenty more to come.

I am delighted the Daily Echo has produced this fantastic book, telling the story of your wonderful, world renowned Orchestra.

I hope you enjoy it and I look forward to seeing you at a Bournemouth Symphony Orchestra concert very soon!

Kirill Karabits

Chief Conductor,
Bournemouth Symphony Orchestra

In association with

bournemouth
symphony orchestra

BSolive.com

Kirill Karabits: Chief Conductor of the Bournemouth Symphony Orchestra since August 2008

3

The Bournemouth Municipal Orchestra circa 1893

Programmes from the early years of the then Bournemouth Municipal Orchestra

1893 to 1939
The opening bars...

"It seems as if the new band will catch on."
That was the verdict of a newspaper reporter after an unknown 24-year-old conducted the first performance of his Bournemouth band with around 30 musicians at the Winter Gardens on 22 May 1893.

It was, by any standards, an understatement.

By the time he had lowered his baton, what would eventually become the world famous Bournemouth Symphony Orchestra was born.

Not unlike the present day, Bournemouth was undergoing significant development.

And part of that, alongside new buildings and the growth of the town as a health resort attracting the rich, famous and sometimes notorious, was the idea of creating a full blown municipal orchestra.

The local council, after acquiring the Winter Gardens, came up with a shortlist of names to get the project underway.

They eventually chose Dan Godfrey, the son of one of the great bandsmen of the day. His father was bandmaster of the Grenadier Guards from 1856-96.

The young Godfrey had returned from South Africa where he managed a touring opera company. He was contracted at £95 a week to lead the new Bournemouth Municipal Orchestra.

He provided a band of 30 musicians, dressed in blue and gold uniforms and pillbox hats.

They made their debut at the old Winter Gardens on Whit Monday.

The all-glass Winter Gardens was not universally admired, nor indeed anywhere near being the world's best concert hall. It was variously nicknamed the Old Greenhouse, the Hothouse, the Conservatory and the Cucumber Frame.

In his 41 years at the head of the Orchestra, Sir Dan Godfrey conducted more than 2,000 symphony concerts until his retirement in 1934.

Under his leadership the Orchestra made its first trips to London (playing at Crystal Palace as part of the Festival of Empire in 1911), released its first records (78rpm recordings on the HMV label in 1914), gave its first concerts on local and national radio and was broadcast far and wide by the British Broadcasting Corporation.

The Crystal Palace performance was the Orchestra's first in London and one of its greatest triumphs.

The Times wrote: "Mr Godfrey has succeeded in making the public take a genuine interest in British music and those who make it.

"That a town like Bournemouth should become one of the most important centres of music in England is a curious commentary on our way of doing things..."

He brought some of the giants of classical music to Bournemouth.

(Continued overleaf)

In association with

**bournemouth
symphony orchestra**

BSOlive.com

Sir Dan Godfrey who led the Orchestra for 41 years

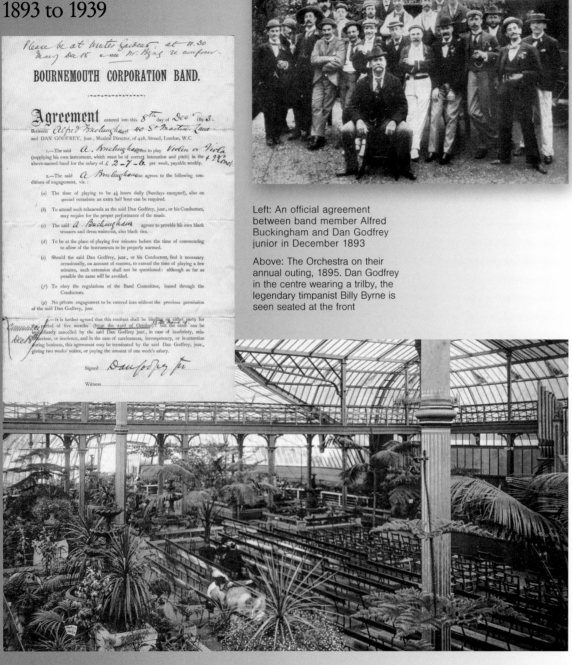

Left: An official agreement between band member Alfred Buckingham and Dan Godfrey junior in December 1893

Above: The Orchestra on their annual outing, 1895. Dan Godfrey in the centre wearing a trilby, the legendary timpanist Billy Byrne is seen seated at the front

Edward Elgar, who epitomised Britain at the height of her imperial glory, conducted a programme of his own music in 1908 and returned a number of times.

In 1910 a concert for the town's centenary brought together Elgar, Hubert Parry (who was born in Bournemouth), Charles Villiers Stanford, Edward German and Alexander Mackenzie.

The list of guest conductors during Godfrey's time is a roll call of legends. The Finnish composer Jean Sibelius, Gustav Holst, Ralph Vaughan Williams, Henry Wood, William Walton, Thomas Beecham and Adrian Boult.

Holst once cycled from London to Bournemouth with a new score but was apparently mistaken for the paperboy by Godfrey's wife.

During the Great War, audiences dwindled but the Orchestra played on and just before the end of hostilities, celebrated its 25th anniversary.

Godfrey was recommended for a knighthood by the Prime Minister, David Lloyd George in 1922 for his "valuable services to British music."

In 1926, members of the Orchestra beat the General Strike by climbing aboard a bus for a concert tour of South Wales.

The Pavilion provided a new venue when it was opened in 1929 by the Duke of Gloucester and from here, BBC broadcasts spread the reputation of the BMO even further. On 21 May 1933, the Pavilion played host to the fortieth anniversary concert. It was relayed across Britain. Sir Dan's legacy was huge.

As a biography at the time of his retirement noted: "He has been most enthusiastic in helping unknown British composers to a hearing, of whom many have become distinguished. He has always been known for sincerity of purpose, if at times unduly frank in his opinions."

It was noted that Sir Dan "took a great interest in social endeavour," something now at the very heart of the BSO's philosophy and remit.

It was estimated that no fewer than 220 British composers had their works performed - around 850 different pieces, of which 116 were first performances.

Of the great symphonic works, the four symphonies of Brahms had 235 performances, Beethoven's *Ninth* 350 and Tchaikovsky's *Sixth* 120.

The role of Bournemouth civic leaders was also noted as forty years of the Orchestra was reflected upon.

"It will surely be interesting to place on record the undoubted important chapter in British music which has been accomplished through the enterprise of the Bournemouth Corporation."

Sir Dan was succeeded by Richard Austin in 1934, the year that Elgar, Holst and Delius died. BSO historian Geoffrey Miller described it as "the saddest of all years for British music." The BSO founder broke down at the podium amid emotional scenes and was supported by his assistant Montague Birch.

Under Austin the BMO continued to flourish.

The popular Sunday concerts were more symphonic and recitals were performed in local schools.

More great names came including Boult and Barbirolli, and Igor Stravinsky conducting a programme that included *The Firebird*.

Austin oversaw the growth of the orchestra to 61 players by 1937. In 1939, at the March Festival, the BMO and the Municipal Choir performed Brahms' *Requiem*.

But everything was soon to change.

The BMO performed a concert on 2 September as the storm clouds gathered. The following day, the war that had threatened for so long finally arrived.

Ladies and gents, in waiting: Early arrivals for the Municipal Orchestra's concert pass the time amidst the tropical greenery of the Winter Gardens

Mr Dan Godfrey junior with the Bournemouth Municipal Orchestra, in their blue and gold uniforms with pillbox hats, when they first played at the Winter Gardens

MASTER MAX DAREWSKI. CONDUCTING.

Top left: Dan Godfrey conducting at the original Winter Gardens, 1905

Above: Master Max Darewski conducting the Orchestra, circa 1900

Inset: The programme of music, 2 June 1900

An exterior picture of the Winter Gardens in 1900

Water music: Entertaining the 1905 summer crowds at the Pier bandstand

1893 to 1939

Top left: The colourful Bournemouth Centenary Fetes programme in 1910

Top centre: Programme for the Orchestra at the Winter Gardens and on the Pier, 1909

Right: W.W. Bennett Senior and Junior who between them were members of the percussion section from the birth of the Orchestra to 1948, seen here in 1908

In 1907 morning and afternoon concerts in the open air of the Bournemouth's Lower Pleasure Gardens were a part of the seasonal programme

1910 sees a notable line up: Left to right, Edward Elgar, Edward German, Dan Godfrey, Alexander Mackenzie, Hubert Parry and Charles Villiers Stanford

1893 to 1939

Top right: A postcard from 1913 showing the exterior of the Winter Gardens

Bottom right: Programme for the Municipal Orchestra at the Winter Gardens and on the Pier 1912

1919 and it's the Orchestra's first tour. Seventeen concerts given over eight days in Pontypridd, Cheltenham and Weston-super-Mare. Coach driver loses his way in fog

The Bournemouth Municipal Orchestra, choir and soloists performing in the Winter Gardens circa 1912

Left: Programme for the 1922 Easter Festival by British Artistes and the Bournemouth Municipal Orchestra. Conductors included Elgar, Wood and Holst

Right: Winter Gardens and Pier programme, 3 June 1922

Far right: 1922 Dan Godfrey and Harold Darke at Sir Dan's investiture at Buckingham Palace

WINTER GARDENS and PIER PROGRAMME

Dan Godfrey with Sir Alexander Mackenzie, Dame Ethel Smyth, Sir Henry Wood and Sir Edward German, all of whom conducted the BMO during the 1922 Easter Festival

Sir Dan Godfrey and musicians enjoy a light moment at rehearsals for the first Easter Festival, 1922

Left: A newspaper cutting in June 1926 with a somewhat understated caption...
'AN INTERESTING GROUP.
An informal picture taken at the recent Bournemouth Festival. Left to right (standing) – Solomon, Sir Dan Godfrey, Gustav Holst; (seated) – Dame Ethel Smyth, Sir A. C. Mackenzie, Isolde Menges'

1928 Winter Gardens: monthly synopsis of coming events at the Winter Gardens for the BMO

The Bournemouth Municipal Orchestra outside the Winter Gardens in 1926

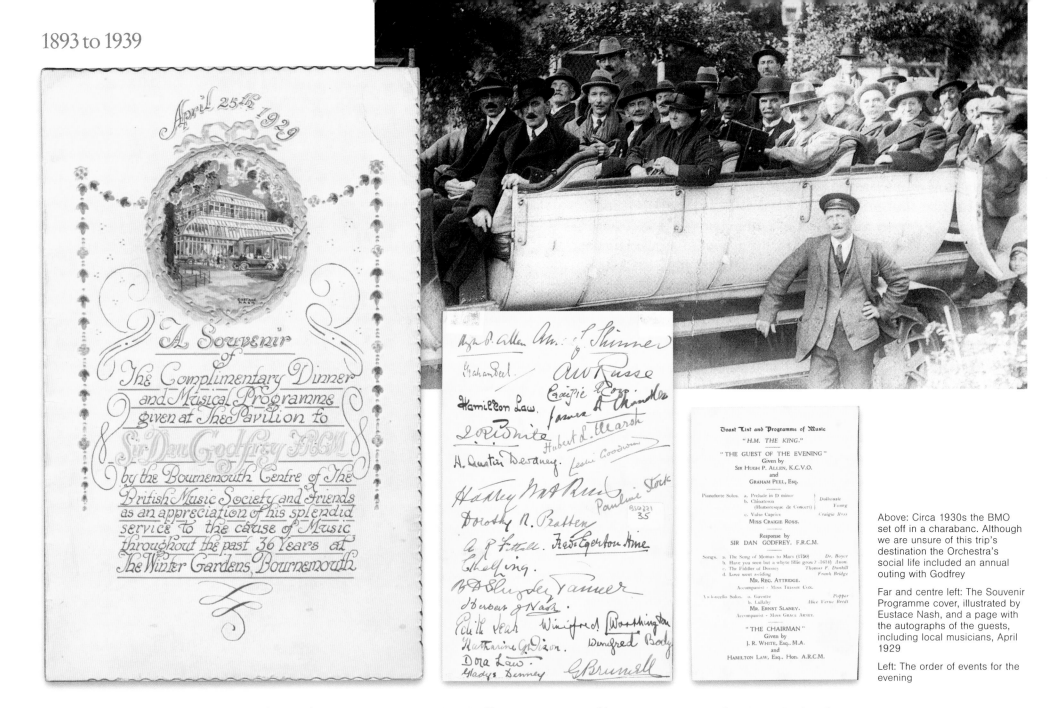

Above: Circa 1930s the BMO set off in a charabanc. Although we are unsure of this trip's destination the Orchestra's social life included an annual outing with Godfrey

Far and centre left: The Souvenir Programme cover, illustrated by Eustace Nash, and a page with the autographs of the guests, including local musicians, April 1929

Left: The order of events for the evening

A Souvenir of a Complimentary Dinner and Musical Programme given to Sir Dan Godfrey in appreciation of his service to music at the Winter Gardens for 36 years

Full house: The captivated and entertained audience of the 1929 Pavilion's opening concert

Out-Door Music in Mid-Winter.

Left and top left: Cuttings from the Orchestra's newspaper publicity, circa 1935

Above: A photo from the Bournemouth Daily Echo front page captioned thus... 'Out-Door Music in Mid-Winter. Scenes such as the above are to be encountered on fine mornings when, as today, a section of the Bournemouth Municipal Orchestra plays in the Pine Walk.' It must be true as the image shows crowds gathered on 7 January 1935!

Right: The label from the Bournemouth Municipal Orchestra's record, *The Dicky Bird Hop* (Gourley arr. Storm), recorded in the Pavilion, Bournemouth, 1934

Richard Austin (main image) took over as Chief Conductor of the Bournemouth Municipal Orchestra in 1934 when Sir Dan Godfrey retired

Summer 1934 and the Bournemouth Municipal Orchestra, led by Sir Dan Godfrey, performs for the crowds at Bournemouth's Lower Pleasure Gardens bandstand

ENGAGEMENT OF MR. RICHARD AUSTIN.

Attracted First by a 'Phone Voice.

AND THEN BY 'CELLO PLAYING.

Cancelled Concert That Led To Meeting With Miss Howell.

THE engagement of Mr. Richard Austin, Director of Music to the Bournemouth Corporation and conductor of the Municipal Orchestra, to Miss Leily Howell, a pretty 22-years-old 'cello soloist, was announced at Bournemouth last night.

Their romance began with a telephone call from Miss Howell to Mr. Austin sometime after the cancellation of a concert at the Pavilion owing to stage alterations last July.

MR. AUSTIN, who is 31 years of age and is being showered with congratulations, told the story in an "Echo" interview to-day, following the announcement of their engagement at a private dinner to members of the Municipal Orchestra last night

"Miss Howell, whom I had never met, rang me up when I was in London and asked for an audition," he said. "She was keen on playing at the Pavilion.

"I rather liked the sound of her

Although the time and place of the wedding have not yet been fixed, the "Echo" understands that it will take place in London.

Since Miss Howell is a Catholic, the ceremony will in all probability be held in a Roman Catholic church in the Sloane Square district.

STUDIED IN PARIS.

Miss Howell, whose family come from Devonshire, recently completed three years' studies under Professor Diran Alexanian, at the Ecole Normale of Music.

She has played in the Pump Room

Romantic note: The official announcement of the engagement of Mr Richard Austin to Miss Leily Howell, cellist, 15 February 1935

Richard Austin with the Bournemouth Municipal Orchestra, 1935

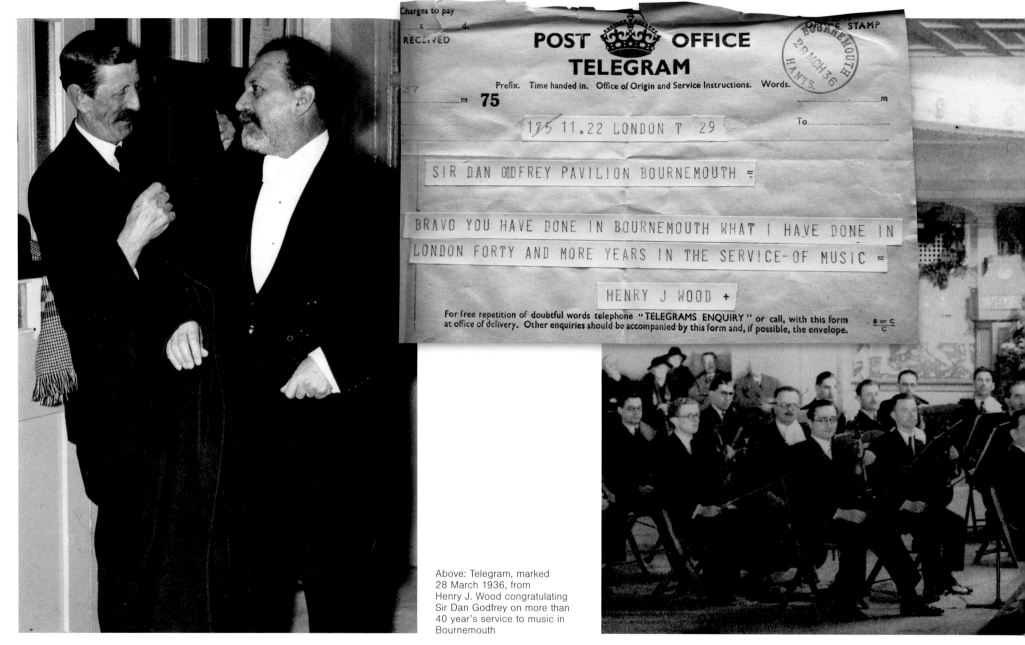

POST OFFICE
TELEGRAM

Charges to pay
s. d.
RECEIVED

OFFICE STAMP
BOURNEMOUTH
29 MCH 36
HANTS.

Prefix. Time handed in. Office of Origin and Service Instructions. Words.

m 75

To

175 11.22 LONDON T 29

SIR DAN GODFREY PAVILION BOURNEMOUTH =

BRAVO YOU HAVE DONE IN BOURNEMOUTH WHAT I HAVE DONE IN
LONDON FORTY AND MORE YEARS IN THE SERVICE-OF MUSIC =

HENRY J WOOD +

For free repetition of doubtful words telephone "TELEGRAMS ENQUIRY" or call, with this form
at office of delivery. Other enquiries should be accompanied by this form and, if possible, the envelope.

B or C
C

Above: Telegram, marked
28 March 1936, from
Henry J. Wood congratulating
Sir Dan Godfrey on more than
40 year's service to music in
Bournemouth

Sir Henry Wood, the famous conductor, being helped with his coat at the Pavilion stage door by Hallkeeper, Mr A. Skeldon, 25 March 1936

Richard Austin and the Orchestra in 1936

Top left: A few BMO musicians playing on the pier, 1939, as part of their duties as civic employees

Left: Sir Dan Godfrey relaxes in a deckchair with a pipe, during his well-earned retirement

The Bournemouth Municipal Orchestra during rehearsals at the Bournemouth Pavilion, 1939

Sun and sandwiches: Musicians of the Bournemouth Municipal Orchestra relaxing on Bournemouth Pier, 1939

The Bournemouth Municipal Orchestra with Conductor, Rudolf Schwarz, in the Winter Gardens Concert Hall, 18 October 1947

Top left: Schwarz and the Winter Gardens Society train, 1948

Above: Rudolf Schwarz wields the baton

Left: The Easter Festival programme, 1956

1940 to 1959
Picking up the baton

The outbreak of war had a big impact on the Bournemouth Municipal Orchestra. There were just 24 players left and Austin resigned early in 1940, disagreeing with the Corporation's policy of cutting down the Orchestra.

But Montague Birch, who had been with the BMO for nearly 30 years, picked up the pieces and the baton and the small group carried on.

The popular Sunday concerts continued as Birch kept the municipal flag aloft. The back row violinist and deputy to both Sir Dan and Austin had well and truly stepped into the breech "admirably maintaining the BMO's great prestige."

In difficult times it was a huge responsibility. Despite all the challenges and tribulations of wartime, the quiet and modest Birch guided the Orchestra to more success.

Audiences grew as servicemen and women came to Bournemouth. Music was alive and well.

The BMO celebrated its Golden Jubilee in 1943. Birch and Sir Adrian Boult, conductor of the BBC Orchestra, shared the conducting at two celebratory concerts on Sunday 23 May. Birch received a standing ovation at both appearances, the Orchestra "augmented by former members and others," and numbering a spirited 55, "conjuring up hopes that an Orchestra of this capacity may be available after the war."

The Echo captured the mood and the importance of the Orchestra in a piece marking the anniversary. It wrote: "In the midst of the most terrible war the world has ever seen, music certainly has its claims as one of the people's greatest standbys and tonics. "And the Municipal Orchestra, which on Sunday celebrates its fiftieth anniversary, holds a proud

place in musical circles for the manner in which, year after year, it provides the people of Bournemouth with all that is best in music, sometimes in the face of very great wartime difficulties."

They proved to be prophetic sentiments. On the very day of the anniversary, Bournemouth suffered its worst bombing raid of the war at the hands of the Luftwaffe. More than 70 people including American, Australian and Canadian troops died in the attacks on the Metropole and Central hotels. Beales was burnt out.

The Orchestra continued recording with Decca. This included Delibes' *Coppelia* and *The Dance of the Hours* by Ponchielli. Seven records were made, all in the Pavilion.

Just before the war, the Corporation had built an indoor bowling green on the site of the old Winter Gardens. The new and not particularly attractive (at least from the outside) building was requisitioned during the conflict by the Air Ministry for use by the Canadian Air Force but then returned to the Council in 1946.

(Continued overleaf)

In association with

ƒ bournemouth
symphony orchestra

BSOlive.com

Montague Birch served the Orchestra in a wide variety of roles including Musical Director

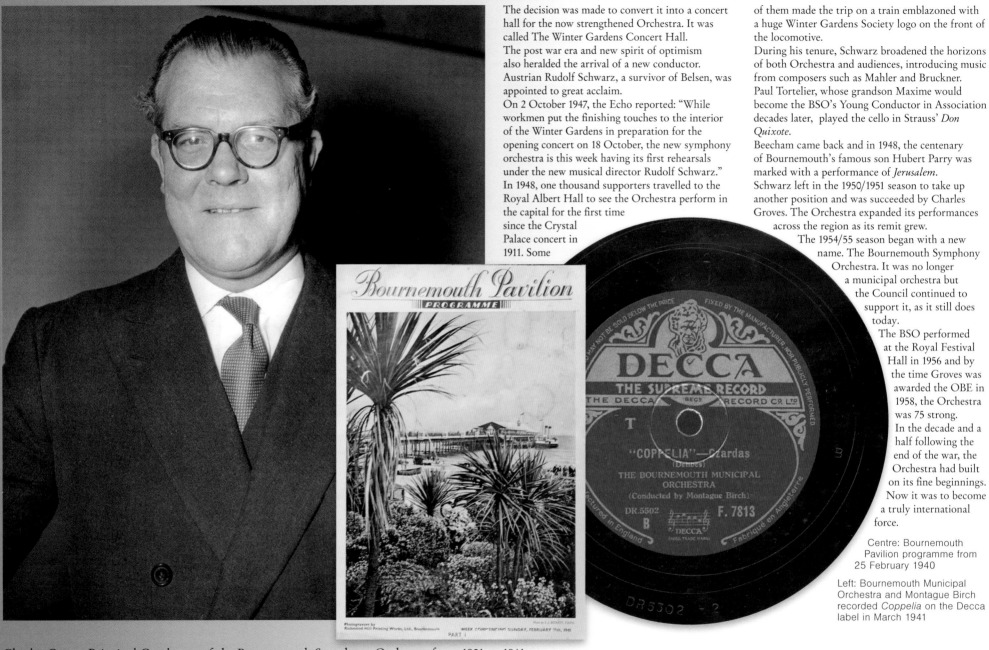

The decision was made to convert it into a concert hall for the now strengthened Orchestra. It was called The Winter Gardens Concert Hall.

The post war era and new spirit of optimism also heralded the arrival of a new conductor. Austrian Rudolf Schwarz, a survivor of Belsen, was appointed to great acclaim.

On 2 October 1947, the Echo reported: "While workmen put the finishing touches to the interior of the Winter Gardens in preparation for the opening concert on 18 October, the new symphony orchestra is this week having its first rehearsals under the new musical director Rudolf Schwarz."

In 1948, one thousand supporters travelled to the Royal Albert Hall to see the Orchestra perform in the capital for the first time since the Crystal Palace concert in 1911. Some of them made the trip on a train emblazoned with a huge Winter Gardens Society logo on the front of the locomotive.

During his tenure, Schwarz broadened the horizons of both Orchestra and audiences, introducing music from composers such as Mahler and Bruckner. Paul Tortelier, whose grandson Maxime would become the BSO's Young Conductor in Association decades later, played the cello in Strauss' *Don Quixote*.

Beecham came back and in 1948, the centenary of Bournemouth's famous son Hubert Parry was marked with a performance of *Jerusalem*.

Schwarz left in the 1950/1951 season to take up another position and was succeeded by Charles Groves. The Orchestra expanded its performances across the region as its remit grew.

The 1954/55 season began with a new name. The Bournemouth Symphony Orchestra. It was no longer a municipal orchestra but the Council continued to support it, as it still does today.

The BSO performed at the Royal Festival Hall in 1956 and by the time Groves was awarded the OBE in 1958, the Orchestra was 75 strong.

In the decade and a half following the end of the war, the Orchestra had built on its fine beginnings. Now it was to become a truly international force.

Centre: Bournemouth Pavilion programme from 25 February 1940

Left: Bournemouth Municipal Orchestra and Montague Birch recorded *Coppelia* on the Decca label in March 1941

Charles Groves Principal Conductor of the Bournemouth Symphony Orchestra from 1951 to 1961

Montague Birch in the Ballroom at the Pavilion, with the Bournemouth Municipal Orchestra. The Orchestra consisted of 61 musicians at the time, 1939/1940 season

Top right: The Bournemouth Municipal Orchestra with their Conductor, Rudolf Schwarz at the opening concert of the new Winter Gardens Concert Hall 18 October 1947

Bottom right: The concert programme for the evening

WINTER GARDENS

WINTER GARDENS
Bournemouth

OPENING · SATURDAY, OCTOBER 18th, 1947

The New Home

MUNICIPAL ORCHESTRA

CONDUCTOR · RUDOLF SCHWARZ

The new-look Winter Gardens where the Bournemouth Municipal Orchestra played for the first time on 18 October 1947

Conductor Rudolf Schwarz conferring with Edward Armstrong, leader, Cedric Morgan and other BMO members over a score in the Winter Gardens, October 1947

Right: Sir Thomas Beecham
rehearsing with the Bournemouth
Municipal Orchestra preparing
for a concert at the Winter
Gardens, 1948

Far right: Rudolf Schwarz goes
through his notes in his Winter
Gardens office, October 1948

Rudolf Schwarz conducting the BMO in the Winter Gardens, the view from the Orchestra looking towards the audience, circa 1948

Alfred Jupp, Edward Armstrong, leader, and Rudolf Schwarz are at the front of the throng as they walk along the platform beside the BMO branded locomotive

WINTER · GARDENS · SOCIETY
BOURNEMOUTH MUNICIPAL ORCHESTRA

Rudolf Schwarz with members of the BMO and their supporters arrive in London for their Royal Albert Hall appearance, 1948

Sections of the Orchestra rehearsing at the Winter Gardens

WINTER GARDENS

General Manager - L. H. HARKER   Manager - S. L. BACON

WEDNESDAY, FEBRUARY 2nd
at 7.30 p.m.

THE AMAZING 11-YEAR-OLD
ITALIAN BOY CONDUCTOR

PIERINO
GAMBA

By arrangement with JACK HYLTON and HAROLD FIELDING

CONDUCTING

THE BOURNEMOUTH
MUNICIPAL ORCHESTRA

(Leader - EDWARD ARMSTRONG)

Overtures : Egmont (Beethoven); William Tell (Rossini)
Beethoven : Fifth Symphony
Schubert : "Unfinished" Symphony

BOOKING OPENS JANUARY 26th, at 10 a.m.

3/-,   4/-,   5/-,   6/-,   7/6,   and   8/6

WINTER GARDENS BOX OFFICE (Telephone 4605)

The amazing Italian boy conductor takes the lead of the Bournemouth Municipal Orchestra at the Winter Gardens, 2 February 1949

Left: The programme announces the presence of the boy prodigy

11-year-old Pierino Gamba weaves his magic

Oct. 1947 - Sept. 1951

RUDOLF SCHWARZ

"Four Years' Achievement"

WHEN Mr. Rudolf Schwarz was appointed Director of Music to the Bournemouth Corporation in September, 1947, and the Municipal Orchestra was brought up to a strength suitable for the performance of major symphonic works the hope was expressed that a new "Golden Age" was dawning for music in Bournemouth. This hope has been more than fulfilled. Nowhere in England—or out of it—has there been a carefully planned series of orchestral concerts comparable in scope, variety, or general level of excellence to those given week in, week out, during the past four years. During this time the number of different works given at symphony and special concerts alone exceeds 650, and these include the majority of the orchestral masterpieces of all periods by composers of all nationalities. Add to this a similar number of works of lighter type given on Saturdays and Sundays and the amount of ground covered is seen to be immense.

The number of works performed for the first time by the municipal orchestra during this period is in the region of 750. Continuing the far-sighted policy of Sir Dan Godfrey, Mr. Schwarz has included at least one work by a British composer in almost every concert. The people of Bournemouth have, in short, been given the opportunity of a musical education which is quite unique.

When I was asked to write analytical notes for the programmes of these Symphony Concerts, Mr. Schwarz specially requested me to give where possible such biographical and historical details as would place the musical works in their proper setting. An opportunity now occurs to attempt a very brief general survey of what has been done.

The birth of the modern orchestra coincides with the perfection of the violin, viola and 'cello which was achieved by the great Italian violin makers at the end of the seventeenth century. Amongst the first writers of "concerti grossi" for a large number of instruments of the violin family are Corelli, Handel and J. S. Bach. Works by all three of these composers have been played at the Symphony Concerts: e.g., Concerto Grosso No. VIII of Corelli "made for the eve of the Nativity"; three Concerti Grossi of Handel, two Overtures, three Suites, an Oboe Concerto and two Viola Concertos. With J. S. Bach other instruments are introduced, and we have had the rare pleasure of hearing all six Brandenburg Concertos, three Suites, three Piano Concertos, three Violin Concertos and a Concerto for Oboe d'amore. Municipal Choir and Orchestra have joined in the B minor Mass and the St. Matthew Passion.

Joseph Haydn has been rightly called the Father of the Modern Orchestra. At least fourteen of his best Symphonies have been performed, including all twelve of the Salomon set (Nos. 93-104). We have heard in addition the 'Cello Concerto. Mozart learnt much from Haydn and in his turn taught him much. Nine of his Symphonies have been performed, eight Piano Concertos, six Concertos for other instruments (violin, bassoon, horn, oboe, flute and harp), seven Overtures, three German Dances, and many operatic Arias.

The symphony reached its zenith with Beethoven, all of whose nine Symphonies have been given several times. Special mention must be made of two outstanding performances of his Choral Symphony during the Festival of Britain with the augmented Municipal Choir. All eleven Overtures, all five Piano Concertos, the Violin Concerto, the Ballet Music from "Prometheus," and the Mass in D have been included in the series.

If Beethoven's treatment of the orchestra may be regarded as a standard, it has been interesting to note the different styles of his successors.

Weber was perhaps the first to use the horns with romantic effect. We have had many magical performances of his Overtures to Oberon, Euryanthe, Der Freischütz, Preciosa and the Ruler of the Spirits.

Schubert gave to his Symphonies a lyrical character; in them delightful melodies swell forth from oboe, clarinet and other wind instruments. Six of his Symphonies, two Overtures, and the Entr'actes and Ballet Music from "Rosamunde" have been played many times. Schumann's orchestration has been much criticized. He keeps the strings hard at it all the time; none the less his four Symphonies, his 'Cello and Piano Concertos contain much noble and romantic music. We have heard them all, as well as the lesser known Overture, Scherzo and Finale.

Mendelssohn is a landscape painter in music. Eight Overtures, three Symphonies, the Violin Concerto, his First Piano Concerto, and some of his music for "Midsummer Night's Dream" have shown how varied are the colours on his palette.

It is natural that Brahms' orchestral style should be modelled on Schumann, whom he admired and loved. His range and grasp of form are much greater than his master's, and his works for orchestra are imperishable.

Mr. Schwarz is a great interpreter of Brahms and has given us the four Symphonies, the Academic and Tragic Overtures, both Piano Concertos, Violin Concerto, the Concerto for Violin and 'Cello, the two Serenades and the Haydn Variations, whilst the Municipal Choir has joined in the German Requiem, the Song of Destiny and the Alto Rhapsody. Other great names in the Austro-German school are Richard Strauss, Wagner, Bruckner and Mahler. We have had superb performances of all Strauss' Symphonic Poems as well as rarer works like the Burlesque for Piano and Orchestra and the Oboe Concerto.

Wagner has had his special concerts with artists such as Kirsten Flagstad and many delightful renderings of the "Siegfried Idyll" linger in the memory.

Bruckner's Third, Fourth and Seventh Symphonies have been played, and of Mahler we have had two memorable performances of "Das Lied von der Erde." In addition Symphony No. 4, "Lieder eines Fahrenden Gesellen" and Lieder from "Des Knaben Wunderhorn" have been given.

Bruch, Goldmark, Humperdinck, Nicolai, Reger and Johann Strauss have all been represented as well as the living composers Hindemith and Hans Gál.

With the rise of the romantic movement came the consciousness in the various nations of Europe of their own musical inheritance and the formation of their own Schools of Composers. Russia is a striking example. Mr. Schwarz has acquainted us with works by Glinka, Borodin (Symphony No. 2 and Overture and Dances from "Prince Igor"), Moussorgsky, Glazounov (Symphony No. 6, Carnaval Overture, Violin Concerto and "Stenka Razine"), and Rimsky-Korsakov. Tchaikovsky has been well represented by all his seven Symphonies (including Manfred), three Piano Concertos and the Fantasie de Concert, the Violin Concerto and Sérénade Mélancholique, the 'Cello Rococo Variations, the Fantasy-Overtures: "Hamlet," "Romeo and Juliet" and "Francesca da Rimini," the Capriccio Italien, the Serenade (Op. 45), the Suite (Op. 55), the Ballet Suites: "Casse Noisette," "Swan Lake" and "The Sleeping Beauty," and the Polonaise from "Eugène Onégin."

Twentieth century Russian composers who have figured on the programmes are Rachmaninov (three Piano Concertos and the Paganini Rhapsody), Stravinsky (Suites from "Petrouchka," "Pulcinella" and the "Firebird"), Prokofiev (Piano Concertos Nos. 1 and 3 and the "Classical" Symphony), Khatchaturian (three Concertos and the Dances from "Gayaneh"), Kabalevsky, Konstantinov, Kopylov, Shostakovitch, Medtner and Mossolov.

Mr. Schwarz has a very warm spot in his heart for Dvořák—the greatest master of the Bohemian School. Of Smetana, its founder, we have heard the Symphonic Poems, "Richard III" and "Vltava," and the Overture, Dances and an Aria from "The Bartered Bride." Dvořák's list is much longer—five

[continued on Page Three of Cover

BOURNEMOUTH MUNICIPAL ORCHESTRA

Leader: EDWARD ARMSTRONG

Conductor: **RUDOLF SCHWARZ**

FAREWELL CONCERT

At the WINTER GARDENS

in the presence of

THE MAYOR AND MAYORESS OF BOURNEMOUTH (Councillor and Mrs. Frank J. McInnes)

Saturday, 29th September, 1951, at 8.0 p.m.

★

Programme

(It is interesting to note that Mr. Schwarz is repeating the programme of his opening concert in October, 1947)

THE NATIONAL ANTHEM

1. OVERTURE, The Mastersingers .. .. *Wagner* (1813-1883)

The colour and pomp of mediaeval pageantry pervade this Overture to the greatest of all Comic Operas. The martial theme of the Mastersingers forms a majestic opening section. This is followed by Walther's "Prize Song," the irreverent mockery of the apprentices and allusions to other characters in the comedy. Finally, all the main themes are combined together, thus bringing the Overture to a joyous conclusion. The Mastersingers of Nuremberg, begun in 1860, was finished in 1867, and was produced at Munich in 1868 under Von Bulow.

2. PRELUDE, à l'Après-midi d'un Faune .. .. *Debussy* (1862-1918)

"On the slopes of Mount Etna a faun—half satyr, half man—lies drowsily in the heat of the noonday sun. Visions of nymphs and naiads bemuse his senses and he even pictures himself in a conquest of the Goddess of Love. Quickly realizing the fate that such impious thoughts will bring upon him, he falls into a voluptuous sleep."

Debussy's delicate scoring suggests—rather than illustrates—the mood of Mallarmé's Eclogue. How languid is the opening flute solo, set off by the quivering summer haze of the muted strings and the drowsy softness of the horns! An oboe solo introduces the faun's musings as he lies half asleep, and a climax is reached. Then the mood of the opening returns and the Prelude concludes with an exquisite coda. Delicate arpeggi on the harp are followed by a magical version of the opening theme for horns over a pedal point and the music dies away into silence.

"L'Après-midi d'un Faune" was completed in 1894.

3. VARIATIONS ON AN ORIGINAL THEME (Enigma) (Op. 36) .. .. .. *Elgar* (1857-1934)

The full title of this work—perhaps the most characteristic of all Elgar's output—is "Variations on an original Theme for Orchestra." On the fly leaf is the dedication: "To my friends pictured within—(Malvern, 1899)," and on the first page of the score, "Variations," and over the opening Andante the word "Enigma." The enigma has never been solved. A spirit of kindly friendship permeates these musical portraits, which caricature so lovingly some humorous trait in the nature of each of the friends whose initials stand at the head of the fourteen variations. To the musical student the work will long serve as a model of writing for the orchestra—each variation containing effects that are both original and charming. The *Theme* (in G minor)—Andante, legato e sostenuto—(molto espress) is characterized by drooping thirds and sevenths, with a middle section rising eagerly, 'ere it falls to allow the opening section to be repeated and ended with a G major chord. It leads straight into

Var. I (L'istesso tempo) bearing the initials C.A.E.—Lady Elgar, whose life Elgar describes as a "romantic and delicate inspiration."

Var. II (Allegro, 3/8). H.D.S.P. (H. D. Steuart-Powell), a pianist who used to join Elgar (violin) and B.G.N. ('cello) in chamber music. The opening staccato figure shows him extemporising at the piano.

Var. III (Allegretto, 3/8). R.B.T. (R. B. Townsend). The bassoons and the oboe represent him taking the part of an old man, with a squeaking voice, in amateur theatricals.

Var. IV (Allegro di molto, 3/4). W.M.B.—a generous but forceful host whom Elgar pictures giving orders to his guests, and then leaving the room with a bang of the door.

Var. V (Moderato, 12/8). R.P.A. (R. P. Arnold), a son of the poet Matthew Arnold. The Theme is given out by the bassoons, while R.P.A's serious comments are in the counter melody on the violins; the whimsical side of his nature is portrayed by the woodwind.

Top left: Bournemouth Municipal Orchestra concert programme 29 September 1951 – Conductor Rudolf Schwarz's Farewell Concert – at the Winter Gardens

Rudolf Schwarz and the BMO at the Royal Festival Hall in 1951

Bournemouth Municipal Orchestra and the Bournemouth Municipal Choir at the Winter Gardens performing John Ireland's *These Things Shall Be*, June 1951

Left: Winter Gardens Society crisis meeting with Sir Adrian Boult, Stanley Arthur, Mrs Percy Dixon (sister of Graham Peel) and Leslie Bickel

Below: Diamond Jubilee concerts 1893 -1953 programme Bournemouth Municipal Orchestra at the Winter Gardens, May 1953

Below: Hastily the title on the first programme for the newly named BSO was changed, you can just see Municipal under Symphony, 24 June 1954

Below bottom: A programme from the inaugural performance of the Bournemouth Symphony Orchestra on 7 October 1954

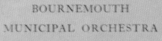

BOURNEMOUTH MUNICIPAL ORCHESTRA

Conductor : *CHARLES GROVES*

Diamond Jubilee Concerts

1893-1953

MAY 22ND, 23RD, 24TH, 25TH
EVENINGS AT 8 P.M.

WINTER GARDENS
BOURNEMOUTH

BOURNEMOUTH SYMPHONY ORCHESTRA

Winter Gardens

THE WESTERN ORCHESTRAL SOCIETY LIMITED

presents

THE INAUGURAL CONCERT

of the

Bournemouth Symphony Orchestra

(LEADER: HUGH MAGUIRE)

Thursday, 7th October, 1954

Bournemouth Municipal Orchestra in the Winter Gardens with Charles Groves and Hugh Maguire (leader). The last concert of the BMO, Easter Sunday 1954

Bournemouth Municipal Orchestra's last performance, Charles Groves conducts, 18 April 1954

Ralph Vaughan Williams visiting the BSO, 1954

Right & top right: Open-air
Concerts programme, 1954

BOURNEMOUTH SYMPHONY ORCHESTRA

Leader: HUGH MAGUIRE.
Conductor: CHARLES GROVES.

Open-Air Concerts

PINE WALK BANDSTAND

2d.

Programme

Week Commencing Monday, 27th September, 1954

Monday Morning, 27th September, at 11.0

1. Overture, Egmont — Beethoven
2. Waltz, The Grenadiers — Waldteufel
3. Three Dances from Nell Gwyn — Edward German
4. Ballet Suite, Sylvia — Delibes
5. Norwegian Dances — Grieg
6. Waltz, The Merry Widow — Léhar
7. Overture, Orpheus in the Underworld — Offenbach

Monday Afternoon, 27th September, at 3.0

1. Overture, Tannhäuser — Wagner
2. Waltz, The Emperor — Johann Strauss
3. Masquerade, The Merchant of Venice — Sullivan
4. March, Washington Post — Sousa
5. Overture, The Arcadians — Monckton and Talbot
6. Slavonic Dances — Dvořák
7. Prelude to Act III, Lohengrin — Wagner

Tuesday Morning, 28th September, at 11.0

1. Overture, The Mikado — Sullivan
2. Concert Waltz No. 1 — Glazounov
3. The Wand of Youth, Suite No. 2 — Elgar
4. March, The Entry of the Gladiators — Fucik
5. Overture, The Flying Dutchman — Wagner
6. Two Spanish Dances — Moszkowski
7. Italian Caprice — Tchaikovsky

Wednesday Morning, 29th September, at 11.0

1. Concert Festival Overture — Horace Shepherd
2. Waltz, The Blue Danube — Johann Strauss
3. (a) Chanson de Matin — Elgar
   (b) Chanson de Nuit
4. Hungarian Rhapsody No. 2 — Liszt
5. Grand March, The Queen of Sheba — Gounod
6. Ballet Suite, Coppélia — Delibes
7. Tone Poem, Finlandia — Sibelius

If wet on Tuesday or Wednesday, performance will be
held in the Pavilion Theatre.

WINTER GARDENS
Monday, 27th September, 1954, at 6.15 & 8.30 p.m.

Jugoslav National Dancers and Singers

in a programme of
GAY and COLOURFUL DANCES and SONGS

Company of 40—200 Brilliant Costumes
Own Orchestra

TWO PERFORMANCES ONLY.

2/6, 4/-, 5/6, 6/6.   Tel. 4605.

1954 sees Charles Groves and the Orchestra go alfresco, in the Pine Walk Bandstand in Bournemouth's Pleasure Gardens

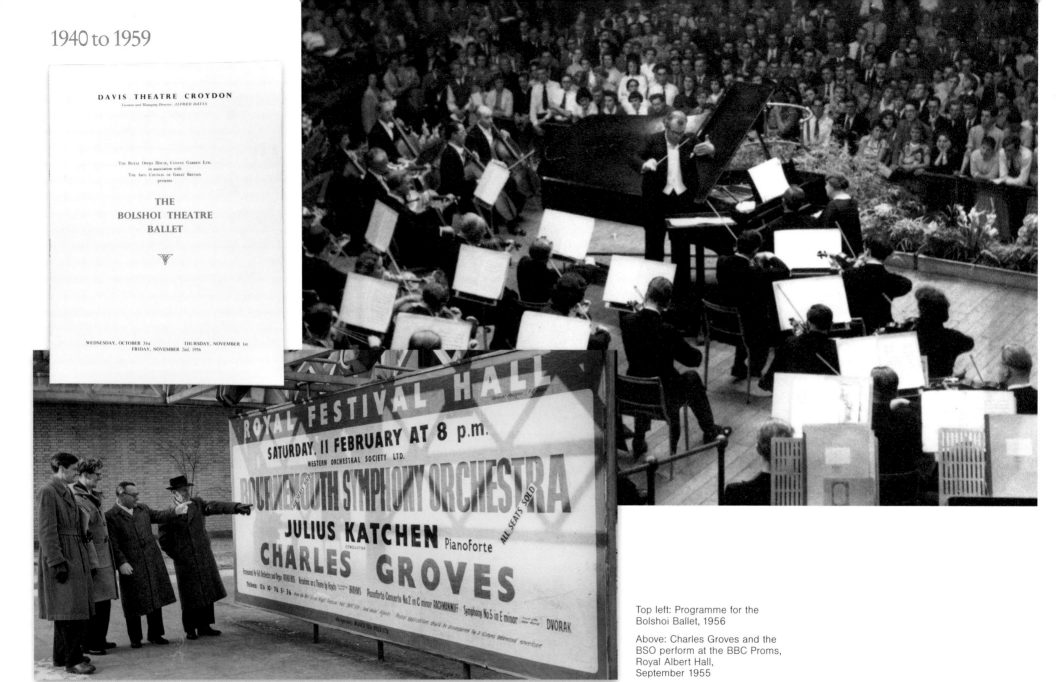

DAVIS THEATRE CROYDON
Licensee and Managing Director: ALFRED DAVIS

The Royal Opera House, Covent Garden Ltd.
in association with
The Arts Council of Great Britain
presents

THE
BOLSHOI THEATRE
BALLET

WEDNESDAY, OCTOBER 31st   THURSDAY, NOVEMBER 1st
FRIDAY, NOVEMBER 2nd, 1956

Top left: Programme for the Bolshoi Ballet, 1956

Above: Charles Groves and the BSO perform at the BBC Proms, Royal Albert Hall, September 1955

Top billing: Bournemouth Symphony Orchestra members check out the promotion for their concert at the Royal Festival Hall, February 1956

Bournemouth Symphony Orchestra rehearsals with the Bolshoi Ballet, 31 October 1956

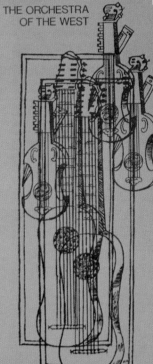

Top right: Constantin Silvestri with the Bournemouth Symphony Orchestra at the Winter Gardens Bournemouth, circa 1960

Right: The cover of a Summer Concert programme, 13 July 1969

Constantin Silvestri with the BSO, 1969

BOURNEMOUTH SYMPHONY ORCHESTRA

Summer Concerts 1969

THE ORCHESTRA OF THE WEST

PROGRAMME

WINTER GARDENS BOURNEMOUTH

Sunday 13th July, 1969 at 8.15 p.m.

ONE SHILLING

1960 to 1969
An electric shock

The 1960s was the decade of Constantin Silvestri, when the BSO won for itself a truly worldwide reputation under the baton of the charismatic Romanian.

The Orchestra became an international force. Already widely admired across Europe, Silvestri's stunning appointment was described as "an electric shock."

He had conducted some of the most famous orchestras in the world, including the Vienna Philharmonic and the Bucharest Philharmonic where he was Chief Conductor, but Silvestri found his greatest happiness with the BSO.

He had the capacity to make an audience sit up and listen.

Silvestri "inspired, thrilled, shocked and started controversy" from the beginning.

He brought glamour.

The Orchestra played all over Britain and toured Europe for the first time, both sides of the Iron Curtain.

But it came at a price. At least in the view of some.

As Geoffrey Miller noted: "Silvestri was accused of tampering with the classics, of gilding the lily, of eccentricity, wilful waywardness, even megalomania.

"He shocked the purist by drastic personal editing of familiar scores, changing note values, phrasing and dynamics to suit his own feelings."

Others said he could do the impossible with an orchestra.

More and more people heard the Orchestra play.

The Echo reported on 28 March 1964: "The busiest summer season in the Bournemouth Symphony Orchestra's history is detailed in the brochure now available. In Bournemouth there are 14 Thursday concerts, 14 Sunday concerts and a special Whit Monday holiday concert."

There would be performances at Crystal Palace, Exeter, Salisbury, Plymouth and Truro and Christchurch Priory.

"A particularly distinguished group of soloists appearing during the season is headed by Yehudi Menuhin, probably the world's best known violinist."

The BSO made its television debut in Winchester Cathedral in 1965, playing two movements from Wagner's *Parsifal* and accompanied the Bolshoi Ballet again at Covent Garden.

The same year during a tour of the UK by the Leipzig Gewandhaus under Vaclav Neumann, the string sections of both orchestras joined together on the Winter Gardens' stage.

Also in 1965, the spectacular European tour saw concerts in Poland, Czechoslovakia, East and West

(Continued overleaf)

In association with

bournemouth
symphony orchestra
BSOlive.com

A portrait of Constantin Silvestri

1960 to 1969

Right: Alceo Gallieria in the midst of a piece, 1960

Below right: A cutting from the Bournemouth Echo in 1961 when Constantin Silvestri (left) became the new Principal Conductor at BSO. He is seen here with Kenneth Matchett (right), General Manager of the Western Orchestral Society, and the Echo's music correspondent Kenneth Williams during a visit to the Echo offices on Richmond Hill, Bournemouth

Germany and Holland and one critic described the BSO "as one of the finest orchestras in Europe."

It was indeed a vintage year which celebrated the centenary of Sibelius and a taste of things to come when the Orchestra played under Finnish conductor Paavo Berglund.

More and more records were made. In 1966 Rimsky-Korsakov's epic *Scheherazade* was recorded by EMI at the Winter Gardens whose unrivalled acoustic made it perfect for orchestral recording. And in November 1966 the BSO played before a vast audience including the Queen and Prince Philip at the Royal Albert Hall. As the Echo reported on 23 November: "The St Cecilia's Day concert for musical charities was a glittering occasion and one of which Bournemouth can be proud, from the moment Silvestri conducted hundreds of musicians in the National Anthem until the audience turned from cheering the Bournemouth players to applaud the Queen and Duke of Edinburgh as they left the Royal box. "Bournemouth had its full part in the ceremonial side. Among the first to be

presented to the Queen and the Duke were six people from the town."

They included the Mayor and Mayoress and Sir Alan Cobham, chairman of the Western Orchestral Society."

1968 saw the 75th anniversary with two successive concerts at the Royal Festival Hall.

The same year, the Bournemouth Sinfonietta came into being.

The first Bournemouth Sinfonietta concerts were performed in Ringwood and Christchurch, under George Hurst and assistant conductor Nicholas Braithwaite. A tour of the west of England followed soon afterwards.

The concept of the Sinfonietta had been considered years before, with a recognition that there needed to be a smaller orchestra to play at some of the venues across the huge region that the BSO served.

The Sinfonietta "soon established itself as a major force in its own right."

The 1960s also saw a new leader appointed, Brendan O'Brien.

Silvestri passed away in 1969 at the age of just 55 and it was truly the end of an era, one still considered with awe in the great history of the BSO.

The whole Orchestra was present at his funeral and he was buried at St Peter's Church, close to the grave of Sir Dan Godfrey.

Rudolf Schwarz conducted Mahler's Seventh Symphony at memorials in Bournemouth, Bristol and Exeter.

There were rumblings in the 60s that the Orchestra might move to Bristol, which some deemed would be a more suitable home, especially given its role across the entire south and south west of England. Bournemouth Council doubled its annual contribution to the BSO to £20,000.

The BSO was "the finest provincial orchestra in the country," an asset the Borough simply could not afford to lose.

Constantin Silvestri with the Bournemouth Symphony Orchestra playing at the Portsmouth Guildhall on 25 June 1962

Charles Groves and Mrs Groves with artists taking part in his farewell concert as Principal Conductor of the BSO at the Winter Gardens, May 1961

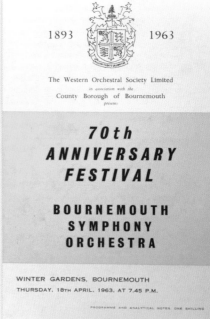

1893   1963

The Western Orchestral Society Limited
in association with the
County Borough of Bournemouth
presents

**70th
ANNIVERSARY
FESTIVAL**

**BOURNEMOUTH
SYMPHONY
ORCHESTRA**

WINTER GARDENS, BOURNEMOUTH
THURSDAY, 18TH APRIL, 1963, AT 7.45 P.M.

PROGRAMME AND ANALYTICAL NOTES, ONE SHILLING

Silvestri with the BSO at a recording session at the Winter Gardens, February 1963

Scaffolding was specially erected in the Winter Gardens to capture the Bournemouth Symphony Orchestra rehearsing in its 'home' under Conductor Constantin Silvestri, October 1962

Bournemouth Symphony Orchestra's new double bass recruits. Left to right, Geoffrey Gray, Graham Beazley, George Folprecht, Lyndon Thomas, May 1965

Above: A good luck horseshoe is presented to BSO leader Gerald Jarvis by Mrs F Lawton, a member of Western Orchestral Society ladies' committee. Watching are Orchestra players Cynthia Mitchell and Raymond Carpenter

Top left opposite: More new recruits Suzanne Bareau, Mary Hillier, Clarissa Melville and Caroline Berthoud, April 1965

Top centre opposite: Principal percussion player Michael Foad with the new 100-guinea single-head bass drum which replaces the smaller one which dates back to the days of Sir Dan Godfrey, March 1965

Top right opposite: David Blenkinsop, BSO concerts manager, left, and an official of HM Customs supervise at Bournemouth Winter Gardens the loading of equipment for the continental tour, September 1965

Bottom right opposite: BSO is considering claiming the title of Britain's best looking orchestra with new recruits, Vivienne Scoot (violin), Elizabeth Earle (viola), Janet Whittaker (viola) and Julie Harvey (violin)

Alderman Reginald Morris, Mayor of Bournemouth and Arthur Thatcher, WOS manager, with BSO players about to embark on the Orchestra's Continental Tour, September 1965

Above: Winchester Cathedral is the venue for this BSO performance, in front of TV cameras in April 1965

Silvestri conducted *Friday Music* from *Parsifal* in Winchester Cathedral. This was the Orchestra's first ever television appearance, Good Friday 1965

The audience is enthralled by Rudolf Schwarz and the BSO performing on the refurbished stage of the Winters Gardens, circa 1965

1960 to 1969

Right: Silvestri on the podium with the BSO in the Winter Gardens, circa 1966

Below centre: Bournemouth Symphony Orchestra programme — The Orchestra of the West 1966/1967 Winter Concert Series

Below right: Giant recording microphones hover over the BSO players at the first recording session for the EMI Studio 2 Stereo series, May 1966

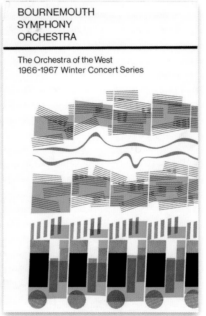

BOURNEMOUTH SYMPHONY ORCHESTRA

The Orchestra of the West
1966-1967 Winter Concert Series

Silvestri concentrates at the control panel to listen to a playback of a recording the Orchestra are making for EMI at the Winter Gardens, January 1967

Her Majesty the Queen and Prince Philip with BSO General Manager Ken Matchett and Mrs Matchett, and Sir Alan Cobham just visible, at the Royal Albert Hall, November 1966

MUSIC
AMID THE POTTED PALMS
and
HOW THE WEST WAS WON

A History of the
BOURNEMOUTH
SYMPHONY
ORCHESTRA

BSO 75
The Western Orchestral Society in association with the County Borough of Bournemouth presents
BOURNEMOUTH
SYMPHONY
ORCHESTRA
1893   1968
75th ANNIVERSARY YEAR
in four
Celebration
CONCERTS
Programme, Analytical Notes, and Historical Details
First Holdings

BSO 75

WESTERN ORCHESTRAL SOCIETY LIMITED

SIR DAN GODFREY
CENTENARY LUNCHEON

THE PAVILION
THURSDAY, 20th JUNE, 1968

Guests of Honour
Sir Michael Tippett, K.B.
The Mayor and Mayoress of Bournemouth
Members of Sir Dan Godfrey's Family

Top: Silvestri, Sir Alan Cobham, Sir John Eden, Madame Silvestri and Sir Michael Tippett at the 75th Anniversary Dinner held at the Pavilion, June 1968 Celebration Concerts

Right: Menu for the Sir Dan Godfrey Centenary Luncheon at the Pavilion

Cutting the cake at the BSO's 75th birthday, Constantin Silvestri including Sir Ralph Richardson and Charles Groves, 1968

Bournemouth Symphony Orchestra at the Winter Gardens, during the 75 years celebrations, with Silvestri conducting, 1968

Paavo Berglund, Principal Conductor of the Bournemouth Symphony Orchestra, in serious mood

SIBELIUS KULLERVO SYMPHONY (First recording) EMI
Swanwhite – excerpts from incidental music / Kuolema – Scene with Cranes
Raili Kostia, mezzo-soprano / Usko Viitanen, baritone
Helsinki University Male Voice Choir (Chorus Master: Ensti Pohjola)
BOURNEMOUTH SYMPHONY ORCHESTRA
PAAVO BERGLUND

Left: Premiere recording by Paavo Berglund and the BSO of Sibelius' *Kullervo Symphony*, 1970

Below: The programme for the Queen's Silver Jubilee Concert in 1977

GH

1977
THE QUEEN'S SILVER JUBILEE

Silver Jubilee Concert
In association with

80p ALL PROCEEDS TO THE SILVER JUBILEE APPEAL

The Carlton Hotel

1970 to 1979
Dark, cool and different

If the 1960s was the decade of Constantin Silvestri, the following one was indisputably that of Paavo Berglund, Principal Conductor from 1972-79.

He was, as was noted at the time "as different from Silvestri as it was possible to be."

As befitting a native of Finland, he was described as "dark and cool."

Berglund, who hailed from Helsinki, began his career as a violinist with the Finnish Radio Orchestra, in time becoming its conductor.

He had previously conducted the BSO during the Sibelius centenary and had indeed met the great composer.

His immediate predecessor was George Hurst, who served as de facto Principal Conductor from 1969 to 1972, without ever being formally appointed to the position.

After Silvestri's death in 1969, Hurst took over responsibility for many concerts under the title of Artistic Adviser until the arrival of Berglund.

The 1970s also saw renewed fears about the future of the BSO.

In July 1971, the Echo reported that the BSO "will play its last note in Bournemouth on Sunday night, unless the council come up with more money."

Kenneth Matchett, General Manager of the Western Orchestral Society said: "If the Corporation care to give us a cheque every Monday morning, it will make certain of a concert that week.

"The Corporation are refusing to accept the true cost of presenting music in Bournemouth. It is a tragedy because the Orchestra has been described nationally as the best in the country."

The same year, more than 100 BSO players boarded a British United BAC 1-11 at Hurn and flew off to play concerts in Cologne and Bonn, the birthplace of Beethoven.

In 1972, the members of the Orchestra provided applause of their own for a man with a remarkable record of musical service.

Douglas Morris, the BSO's Librarian – the person who ensures the players have the right music in front of them at each concert – retired after having served in that post since 1939.

Mr Morris was preceded as Librarian by his father, a bassoonist with the Orchestra from 1924 until his own retirement.

In 1973, the man who had done at least as much as any single individual to ensure that Bournemouth kept its musical tradition alive through the previous two decades returned to his old Winter Gardens rostrum.

Sir Charles Groves made his first trip back since being awarded a knighthood in 1972.

As the Echo reported: "If the face has changed, largely through the addition of a beard, the view of

(Continued overleaf)

In association with

bournemouth symphony orchestra

BSOlive.com

George Hurst conductor of the Bournemouth Symphony Orchestra and Bournemouth Sinfonietta

that broad back and those expansive gestures was a reminder to many in the audience of years of trial and triumph through which Charles - as he is always remembered - led us."

A year after he stepped down as Prime Minister, Edward Heath, conducted the BSO.

The occasion, in October 1975, was the gala concert for the 'Housing for the Orchestra' appeal to provide a home within the new centre for the arts at Poole.

Mr Heath recalled cycling from Southampton to Bournemouth as a boy to hear the BSO under Sir Dan Godfrey. "It is a joy to work with your Orchestra. It is young, it is enthusiastic."

The guest of honour at the event was Lord Mountbatten of Burma: "At times like these we must hold on to our culture," he said.

Berglund's time included the commercial recordings, which have acquired iconic status, of the complete symphonies of Sibelius for EMI.

Berglund is widely regarded to have raised significantly the BSO's performing standards.

Roger Preston, Co-Principal cello said: "I joined the BSO as much because I had seen and heard them play under Berglund.

"Many of his comments, criticisms and demands are as fresh in my mind today as though it was only yesterday.

"I particularly loved it when he used to say: 'Violins, you play like in a telephone box.' In other words use more bow."

Roger added: "He remains for me, one of the best, if not the best conductor I have ever played for."

One of the many high points for members of the Orchestra was a tour of Finland in 1976, which featured performances at the Helsinki Festival and at the world's northernmost concert venue.

In 1978, the BSO played ten concerts at the Hong Kong Festival under Berglund.

The same year, the new Poole Arts Centre opened in the town centre and the Western Orchestral Society moved its offices from Gervis Place.

The Orchestra performed its first concert at the new concert hall in September with Prince and Princess Michael of Kent in the audience.

It was an immense occasion with five conductors who had moulded the story over the previous 30 years (Groves, Hurst, Schwarz, Montgomery and finally Berglund) sharing the rostrum.

In the midst of much change, the BSO gained a new conductor, the young Israeli, Uri Segal.

At the same time, the Friends of Bournemouth Orchestras was formed.

In March 1979 HM the Queen and Prince Philip dropped into a rehearsal before an invited audience at the Wessex Hall, as part of a visit to Poole.

Left: A farewell wave from some of the BSO players as they board their BAC 1-11 for the flight to Cologne

Right: The Bournemouth Symphony Orchestra flew out from Hurn Airport on their short trip to the continent. The girls they left behind - orchestra wives and other members of their families were at the airport to see the players off, January 1971

General Manager Kenneth Matchett wishing bon voyage to the BSO with Douglas Kingsbury, Chairman of the Western Orchestra Society, January 1971 (main image)

George Hurst and the Bournemouth Symphony Orchestra are seen here playing to 5,000 people in the De Doelen Hall at Rotterdam during their European tour, 1971

Above: Rudolf Schwarz in action with the BSO. They are rehearsing at a Poole College annex on Constitution Hill, which they have been offered until the Orchestra breaks for its summer holiday, July 1971

Dumbo the baby elephant from International Circus causing pandemonium among the symphonium at Bournemouth Winter Gardens with Harpist Morfen Edwards, December 1975

Paavo Berglund and the BSO at the Royal Festival Hall, 1972

Top right: Maxim Shostakovich, Russian conductor and son of the distinguished composer, shakes hands with Bournemouth Symphony Orchestra leader Brendan O'Brien before a rehearsal for a Winter Gardens concert. The concert is one of a series known as 'Days of the Music of the USSR' being given by leading Russian musicians with British Orchestras, November 1972

Left: Demonstrators line up with their banners at the Winter Gardens. Concertgoers on the way to a Winter Gardens performance of the Soviet music played by the Bournemouth Symphony Orchestra passed demonstrators carrying posters drawing attention to the predicament of Jews and other minorities in Russia, November 1972

Far left: Paavo Berglund in action

Ron Goodwin, John Butterworth, Kenneth Matchett and Dennis Wise at the retirement of John Butterworth, summer 1972 (top left)

Studio portrait taken of the BSO with Paavo Berglund, in Southern TV studios, circa 1975

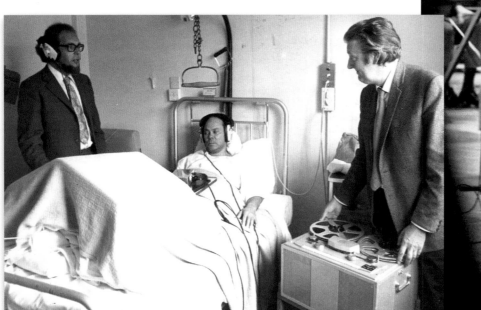

Above: Martin Jones, left, who was appointed co-leader of the BSO, talks to Paavo Berglund at a rehearsal, May 1973

Top centre: Paavo Berglund OBE, an image shot by Echo photographer Harry Ashley as part of a character study, August 1973

Bottom centre: In 1973 BSO conductor Paavo Berglund was hospitalised after being seriously injured in a motor accident. EMI producer David Mottley and engineer Stuart Eltham had to bring recording equipment to Boscombe Hospital.
A room off Ward 21 became a recording studio for an hour!

Paavo Berglund with the BSO at one of the many recording sessions they had at the Southampton Guildhall, January 1973 (right)

Listening to a playback, cellist Paul Tortelier studies the score while Conductor Paavo Berglund, extreme left, listens intently at the Guildhall, Southampton, January 1973

Above: Tikhon Khrennikov, who played his Second Piano Concerto with the BSO. He is seen here at the piano with BSO Conductor Paavo Berglund during a break in the Winter Gardens rehearsals, October 1975

Left: Former Prime Minister Edward Heath conducted the Bournemouth Symphony Orchestra as part of the Gala Concert and supper for the Housing the Orchestra appeal to provide a home for the BSO and Sinfonietta within the new Poole Arts Centre, October 1975

Rudolf Schwarz conducting the BSO with Brendan O'Brien leader in Bournemouth Pavilion Gala Concert, October 1975

Bournemouth Symphony Orchestra's performance at the Royal Festival Hall, London, August 1976

Top Left: Moving day for BSO library to a new home at the Poole Arts Centre. Nicholas Raine, BSO Marketing Manager found an African drum which belonged to Sir Dan Godfrey

Left: Among the now empty archives of the music library Moira Webber, Assistant Librarian and Keith Whitmore, General Administrator, found a copy of Haydn's *Farewell Symphony*, February 1978

Above: Mr Keith Whitmore shows the Chinese banner he brought back from the BSO's Hong Kong trip to two of the girls who stayed behind, Marion Aston (left) and Karen Taylor, 1978

The Orchestra took part in ten concerts as part of the Hong Kong Arts Festival. Akeo Watanabe conducts the BSO, February 1978 (main image)

The BSO's first rehearsal in their new home in the Wessex Hall at Poole Arts Centre, under guest conductor Vernon Handley, March 1978

Left: Prince Michael of Kent, Lady Eden, Sir John Eden, and the Mayor of Poole at the concert

Right: The Queen conversing with Arthur Davidson during the Royal Visit to Poole, April 1979

Below right: Programme for the Royal Gala concert at Poole Arts Centre, 17 September 1978

Bottom right: Paavo Berglund Principal Conductor 1971-1979

Prince and Princess Michael of Kent were in the audience as the Bournemouth Symphony Orchestra gave the first in a series of Royal Galas in Poole, September 1978

As part of their visit to Poole, HM the Queen and the Duke of Edinburgh heard the BSO rehearse at Poole Arts Centre, and were introduced to David Shean, April 1979

Left: BSO demonstration outside
Poole Arts Centre, September 1980

Below: Andrew Litton directing the
Orchestra

Right: Cutting from the Evening Echo
announcing Uri Segal's arrival as
conductor of the BSO, September
1980

Far right: Uri Segal in action during
his two seasons with the Orchestra

New conductor opens season with BSO

THE Bournemouth Symphony Orchestra's new principal conductor Uri Segal this week starts a season in which he will conduct the orchestra in Germany, Scotland and the North of England as well as on their regular "circuit" in their own region.

He will be taking the orchestra on their tour of Germany next spring, and on tours in this country.

His first concert as principal conductor will be at the Winter Gardens on Thursday, and he is meeting the Friends of Bournemouth Orchestras at a dinner tonight.

Apart from his Bournemouth appointment, Segal is also chief conductor of the Philharmonia Hungarica. He won one of the top international conducting competitions in America in 1969, and has since conducted many of the world's leading orchestras.

In the continuing crisis over the Bournemouth Sinfonietta, a statement today by the management of the Bournemouth Orchestras says that musical life in many towns in the south and west is still threatened.

They say the £7,000 response so far to the appeal fund set up by the Friends of the Bournemouth Orches-

match pound for pound any increase which local authorities agree in their aid to the orchestras this year up to a maximum of £15,000.

But of the 52 authorities to which this applies, only a few have so far agreed increases, so the full potential of the Arts Council may not be realised.

● URI SEGAL

Kees Bakels conducting Rimsky-Korsakov's *Easter Festival Overture*. The BSO and the Bournemouth Youth Orchestra together for a concert to launch a Music in the Community project, July 1988

1980 to 1989
Russian masterpieces

The 1980s marked a decade of change for the BSO but one that was filled with some of the most memorable events of its modern history.

From the young Israeli Uri Segal who stayed for just two seasons, the Russian Rudolf Barshai, a world-renowned pupil of Dmitri Shostakovich, to the legendary young American Andrew Litton, the Principal Conductor appointments varied.

However it was a decade when the community's support was unfaltering and proved instrumental to the Orchestra's success.

A new support group was born called Friends of the Bournemouth Orchestras. The network spanning the south west became crucial in providing vital long-term financial support and played a major part in preserving the musical heritage of the region.

In 1981, the BSO toured Switzerland, Austria, Germany and Finland, in what would be one of the most memorable tours in its history.

That July, the Orchestra was reunited with its former Principal Conductor Paavo Berglund to play a Sibelius symphony cycle at the Savonlinna Opera Festival in Finland which he described as "among the best concerts that I ever have conducted." Critics of the televised concert agreed too.

The Echo reported on 15 July 1981 how audiences there demanded up to three encores. It read: "Critics reckoned the performances the BSO gave under their former Principal Conductor Paavo Berglund, of the seven Sibelius symphonies, were the best they had ever heard – this in a country where Sibelius' music is very much the staple diet." On its return, the BSO continued to hit headlines but this time it was a royal occasion.

The BSO and Bournemouth Sinfonietta, whose reputation as a first class chamber orchestra grew daily, were chosen to make recordings on behalf of the town as an official wedding present for Prince Charles and Lady Diana Spencer.

The record, which included a rendition of Tchaikovsky's *1812 Overture*, was put in a case, mounted in goatskin and calf-lined by a specialist book binder before it was taken to Buckingham Palace.

In 1982, Rudolf Barshai was appointed as Principal Conductor, beginning a Russian period for the BSO which was enriched by his special knowledge of Shostakovich and of contemporary Russian masters. After a highly successful period as a world-class viola player, Barshai founded the Moscow Chamber Orchestra in 1955.

As the Echo reported on 29 October 1982 following his debut: "Bournemouth will enhance its reputation as a centre of distinguished music-making under the regime of Rudolf Barshai. "That was made crystal clear in Barshai's first Winter Gardens concert last night."

The following week, news had spread and the

(Continued overleaf)

In association with

bournemouth
symphony orchestra
BSOlive.com

World-renowned Conductor Rudolf Barshai

concert hall was full.

On 5 November 1982 the Echo reported: "It needs little critical acumen to realise that, in Barshai, Bournemouth has a conductor of interpretive genius and one for whom its Orchestra members will play their hearts out."

Play their hearts out, they certainly did. The Orchestra's 90th anniversary was marked with a Royal Festival Hall concert, an EMI birthday disc of recordings from 1930-1981 and a televised gala concert at the Bournemouth Pavilion. Bass Ten was born – a group of 10 BSO players who all played tunes on just one double bass. Initially formed as a fundraiser for the Friends of the Bournemouth Orchestras as a way to safeguard its future, the group soon found themselves in the Guinness Book of Records as well as numerous high-profile TV appearances, even setting a record of 18 people to play the one instrument on BBC1's Record Breakers programme. At home, community efforts intensified. In 1987 and 1988, educational and community initiatives were launched including the popular 'Mega Music Shows'.

Led by BSO Conductor Richard McNicol,

these Family Concerts held at the Winter Gardens saw hundreds of children playing alongside the professionals, 10-year-olds invited to conduct the Orchestra and scores of youngsters even playing on BSO members' valuable instruments.

It was 1988 which saw one of the Orchestra's most memorable appointments – Andrew Litton who became the first American and the youngest Principal Conductor of the BSO.

He started his conducting career in Bournemouth with a highly successful series of recordings for Virgin Classics including a complete Tchaikovsky Symphony set.

The unique chemistry Litton is famed for sharing with the Orchestra, which would later earn him the prestigious title of BSO Conductor Laureate, was born. The love affair began.

Litton said on his appointment: "There was an immediate sort of chemistry which I have since grown very spoiled by. I find it on very few occasions, and I have been told that I will by others who are much more experienced.

"Everyone on the platform there has the same desires as I do to make the most of each moment."

Above right: Principal Conductor Andrew Litton

Left: BSO Family Concerts, March 1988

Brendan O'Brien with an 'apprentice' closely watching his technique (main image), October 1989

The Bournemouth Symphony Orchestra and Chorus in the Poole Proms at Wessex Hall, circa 1980

POOLE Proms 1980 BOURNEMOUTH Symphony Orchestra BOURNEMOUTH Sinfonietta Wessex Hall Poole Arts Centre Saturday, 30 August at 7.30 SPONSORED BY SOUTHERN TELEVISION

Far Left: Demonstrations outside Poole Arts Centre. Two of the Orchestra's violinists, Christine Mallow and Juliet Slade, take part in the impromptu concert highlighting the plight of the members, September 1980

Above centre: Poole Proms programme, August 30 1980

Above: Uri Segal with the BSO during his two seasons with the Orchestra

Demonstrations outside Poole Arts Centre over the financial difficulties facing the Bournemouth Orchestras. Conductor Owain Arwel Hughes lends his support, September 1980

Young BSO fans voice their support, September 1980

Far Left: Ten musicians from BSO who staged a stunt to raise funds for the Orchestra, appeared on BBC Record Breakers. Pictured left to right at back are Peter Witham, Sidney Todd and Michael Humphrey. At the front are Donald MacDonald, Roger Preston, Jonathan Taylor, Clive Brown, Andrew Clunies-Ross, Mike Welsby and Colin Verrell, December 1981

Centre left: Mayor of Bournemouth Cllr Norman Day at Hurn Airport to see the Bournemouth Symphony Orchestra off on their 1981 tour, their first overseas trip since 1978. The Orchestra were also set to visit Finland during the summer

Left: Poole Proms programme, 6 September 1981

POOLE Proms

1981

programme

Wessex Hall Poole Arts Centre
Sunday 6 September 7.30 pm

BOURNEMOUTH
Symphony
Orchestra &
Sinfonietta

The Bournemouth Symphony Orchestra set out from Hurn Airport on a trip which would see concerts in Germany, Switzerland and Austria, March 1981

Uri Segal conducting the Bournemouth Symphony Orchestra during a Southern Television recording, circa 1981

Full Orchestra rehearsal with Rudolf Barshai, January 1983

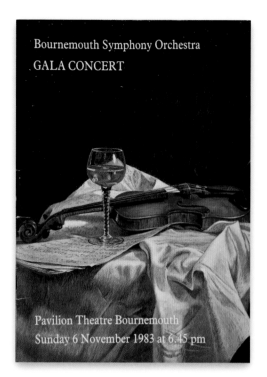

Above left: A portrait image of Rudolf Barshai, BSO Principal Conductor

Above: 6 November 1983 Gala Concert programme

Left: Sir Charles Groves regularly returned to Bournemouth Winter Gardens as a guest conductor. His return on 27 January 1983 held a special significance as it was the Incorporated Society of Musicians' Centenary Year and Sir Charles was their Centenary President

Rudolf Barshai and the Bournemouth Symphony Orchestra, circa 1982

Above: When the Bournemouth Symphony Orchestra gave a free concert at Bournemouth Winter Gardens a queue for the best seats soon built up, circling the building. Buskers Mick Ryan and Ted Street entertain the queue, July 1983

Left: Mike Nutt, the marketing manager of the BSO, sailed around the pier to promote the Summer Pops at the Winter Gardens in August 1985

Rudolf Barshai after signing a new contract as BSO conductor with David Richardson (left), WSO Chairman Nigel Beale (right) and Stephen Lumsden (back centre), November 1984

Swapping piccolos for pads and strings for stumps, the Bournemouth Symphony Orchestra took to cricket at Winton Recreation Ground, August 1984

Right: Spring Serenade Gala Concert programme cover, May 1985

Below: Rudolf Barshai conducting during one of the Orchestra's rehearsals, 1985

CO-OPERATIVE CONGRESS 1985

SPRING SERENADE
INTERNATIONAL GALA CONCERT
Winter Gardens Bournemouth
Monday 27th May 8pm

Bournemouth Symphony Orchestra
Conducted by Kenneth Alwyn
with Helen Field (soprano)
Keith Lewis (tenor)

Sponsored by the Co-operative Movement co-op

After 14 years at the Winter Gardens, Ron Goodwin appears at the Windsor Hall, Bournemouth International Centre to conduct the BSO in his annual Christmas show (main image)

Rudolf Barshai and BSO at Wessex Hall, Poole Arts Centre

Above: Principal Conductor Rudolf Barshai conducts Bournemouth Symphony Orchestra at the Wessex Hall, Poole Arts Centre, February 1986

Left: World famous American jazz drummer Louie Bellson celebrates Independence Day making his debut with the BSO at the Winter Gardens, July 1986

Barry Latchem and Alison Myers get a little help in the Family Concert rehearsals from Magda and Tom Lowes and Brian Heppenstall, November 1986 (left)

Christopher Seaman conducting the Bournemouth Symphony Orchestra in TVS Studios, June 1986

Left: Holidaymakers were stopped in their tracks when the BSO serenaded them from the Noddy train in July 1987

Bottom left: Child prodigy 14-year-old Corey Corevsek, rehearsing with the BSO for two concerts in Bristol and the Royal Festival Hall, London, January 1987

Bottom centre: Stargazer Patrick Moore and percussionist Mike Chesters during rehearsals for the BSO charity concert in 1987

Bottom right: Former Prime Minister Edward Heath conducts the Bournemouth Symphony Orchestra. Completing two days of extensive rehearsals, he opens the town's Summer Pops series of concerts and conducts the BSO through Tchaikovsky's *Symphony No. 5* and Grieg's *Piano Concerto* at the Winter Gardens, July 1987

Schnauzers Charlie Farley and Huggy Bear promote the Bournemouth Symphony Orchestra Summer Pops 1987 series of concerts (top left)

Brendan O'Brien, bottom left, keeps an eye on guest conductor, Bournemouth Mayor Cllr Dan Crone at the BSO's New Year's Day concert with conductor Carl Davis, January 1987

Top left, left and below: An inspired musical experiment got off to a thunderous start at Bournemouth Winter Gardens, as the BSO and the Bournemouth Youth Orchestra get together for a concert to kick off a Music in the Community project, July 1988

Bottom row: Harry Redknapp, amongst others, lends a hand in the BSO Family Concerts, March 1988

Images from a series of concerts during the 1988 Music in the Community project

Members of the BSO dressed in Magic of Vienna mood with Melinda Fraser, Academy of Dance Stage School Principal, as part of the Summer Serenade season, July 1988

Above: Bournemouth Symphony Orchestra with Paul Daniel as guest conductor, May 1989

Left: BSO Family Concert. Pictured are four children being taught how to play the flute and recorder, January 1989

Right: 1989/1990 season programme cover

BOURNEMOUTH SYMPHONY ORCHESTRA

PROGRAMME

1989/90

SYMPHONY

Bournemouth Symphony Orchestra cellist Philippa Eggington (right), May 1989

Richard McNicol and the BSO players take a bow at the end of the Evening Echo sponsored Family Concerts, January 1989

CONCERT PROGRAMME

1990/1991 SEASON

Blowing their trumpets, part of the brass section of the BSO in a series of portraits in 1996 (above)

1990 to 1999
Musical superpowers

If one decade could be truly said to signal the arrival of the BSO on the global stage, it was surely the 90s.

The Orchestra was conducted by Andrew Litton until midway through the decade and then by the brilliant Yakov Kreizberg into the next century. And it performed with a host of international stars including Luciano Pavarotti.

The BSO made its debut at New York's Carnegie Hall (Litton was born in the city in 1959) and also performed at some of Europe's most famous venues including the Musikverein in Vienna and the Royal Concertgebouw in Amsterdam. And memorably too in Paris.

Closer to home the 90s saw the beginning of the popular gala and outdoor concerts with fireworks and even greater exposure on the BBC and Classic FM.

It also saw a huge but ultimately unsuccessful public campaign to 'Save the Winter Gardens' after Bournemouth Council announced it could not afford to keep the concert hall going.

The decade opened with Kees Bakels becoming the chief guest conductor and 1991 saw six performances of Verdi's *Falstaff* in Paris.

Sir Charles Groves passed away in 1992. Celebrations at the end of the Bournemouth International Festival turned to sadness at the news. Tributes poured in for the 77-year-old who guided the Orchestra through its transition from the Bournemouth Municipal Orchestra to the Bournemouth Symphony Orchestra.

Two thousand people, the Orchestra, and a huge choir at the Winter Gardens paid their respects. Sir Charles had been a father figure, a friend and

"always a magical figure on the rostrum." During difficult times and with threats of extinction, he kept the BSO together.

As the Evening Echo reported: "Without the determination and sheer force of his personality there would have been no Bournemouth Symphony Orchestra to celebrate its centenary next year."

But the following year did indeed see many celebrations to mark the 100th birthday of the Orchestra, an immense achievement.

The focal point of the year was the Mahler concerts with a memorable *Resurrection Symphony* at the Royal Albert Hall in May.

A star studded line-up was assembled to celebrate the anniversary, including Kiri te Kanawa, Mstislav Rostropovich, Itzhak Perlman, John Williams and James Galway.

Adding his own tribute, Prime Minister John Major described the BSO as "one of the country's most distinguished musical institutions, a great orchestra."

(Continued overleaf)

In association with

**bournemouth
symphony orchestra**
BSOlive.com

Andrew Litton conducts the Orchestra during the 1991 summer season

Andrew Litton was very proud to be the Principal Conductor in the centenary year.

In 1994, HRH Princess Alexandra became the patron of the BSO. The Orchestra was recognised with an award from the Royal Philharmonic Society and undertook a hugely successful tour of the United States.

Despite the successes, the Orchestra posted a deficit of £213,000. Former Heritage Secretary, David Mellor, called for better funding and described the BSO as "heroic."

The Orchestra performed Verdi's *Requiem* with Luciano Pavarotti at Wembley.

Andrew Litton stepped down in 1995.

His period as Chief Conductor was regarded as a momentous period in the history of the BSO and the musicians and audiences retain a particular affection for him.

He took the BSO to new and dizzying heights and had produced 14 recordings.

He said at the time: "This was the first orchestra I ever conducted that actually made me feel that what I was doing meant anything.

"It started something for me that remains special to this day. It's truly a joy to have a relationship with musicians like this. There's nothing else like it in the world."

Litton's relationship with the Orchestra was not to end with this chapter in his career. It is still a close one.

He regularly returns as a guest conductor and is the BSO's Conductor Laureate.

Russian-born Yakov Kreizberg took the helm in 1995. The charismatic Kreizberg brought with him the ability to infuse music with a dramatic power and an unrivalled attention to detail.

The superlatives flowed.

One reviewer wrote in the conductor's last year with the BSO: "After the interval he conducted from memory the greatest live performance of Shostakovich's *Symphony No. 5* I have ever heard. Utterly faithful to the letter of the score, which is so rarely the case, he and the Orchestra were fully at one with the spirit of this original masterpiece."

He had the ability and passion to "mould an ensemble of intense musical and dramatic presence."

The BSO toured Germany and Austria the following year, featuring that debut in Vienna.

The second US tour in 1997 saw the famous first appearance at New York's Carnegie Hall. Kreizberg also took the Orchestra to the Royal Concertgebouw in Amsterdam.

The year saw Bryn Terfel win the BSO's first Grammy with a recording with the Bournemouth Symphony Chorus, of *Belzhazzar's Feast*.

Brendan O'Brien retired after an incredible 29 years as leader.

The BSO linked up with its first corporate benefactor in 1998, the Portman Building Society, and the same year undertook a sell out national tour with Lesley Garrett.

In 1999, there was a three day, highly acclaimed residency for the BSO at the Musikverein in Vienna. On a national level and in an unprecedented move, the Arts Council announced that every symphony orchestra in the country would have its debts written off.

It would be, said the Council, a fresh start.

The 90s also had many other highlights.

Delius' *Mass of Life* was performed at St Paul's Cathedral under Richard Hickox and the Orchestra also gave the first complete cycle of Vaughan Williams' Symphonies at the Barbican and live on BBC Radio 3.

Kreizberg's tenure ended in 2000.

He passed away in 2011 aged 51 and was buried in Vienna with the inscription Musik war mein leben... Music was my life.

Principal Conductor of the BSO Yakov Kreizberg pictured in 1996 (main image); Rehearsals with Pavarotti and the 700 member World Festival Choir, at Wembley Arena, 1994 (bottom right)

Luciano Pavarotti rehearsing at the Wembley Arena, London, with conductor Gustav Kuhn and the Bournemouth Symphony Orchestra, March 1994

Right: BSO musicians (left to right: Roger Preston, Richard Vaughan-Thomas, Marina Finnamore and Andrew Langley) who ran the 1991 London Marathon to raise money for Orchestra funds

Top right: Evening Echo sponsored Fairground Attractions, part of the BSO Family Concerts, March 1990

Roy Castle joins youngsters for a fun-packed Evening Echo sponsored Mega Music Concert conducted by Jonathan Grieves-Jones, March 1991

Stars of BBC comedy *Bread* Kenneth Waller, left, Jean Boht, centre, and Ronald Forfar, right, with BSO musicians Enid Hughes and Jillian Carter. Conductor Carl Davies looks on, August 1990

Left: Sir Charles Groves returned to lead the BSO for the Gala Concert at the Bournemouth International Festival which featured Paul Patterson's Concerto for Orchestra, Elgar's Cello Concerto with Julian Lloyd Webber as soloist and William Walton's *Belshazzar's Feast* with Baritone David Wilson-Johnson and the Bournemouth Symphony Chorus, June 1991

Right: The Right Honourable Edward Heath MP MBE with BSO Principal Flautist, Karen Jones, who he sponsored through the Orchestra's Sponsor a Chair scheme, June 1991

Julian Lloyd Webber playing with the BSO during the 1991 Bournemouth International Festival, June 1991 (main image)

Julian Lloyd Webber and Sir Charles Groves launched the 1991 Bournemouth International Festival, 8 June, seen here with the Orchestra during rehearsals

Left: Mega Music with BSO and the Evening Echo, 1991

Right: BSO Family Concert, March 1992

Below right: Andrew Litton in the moment during Bolero in the Park, Meyrick Park, July 1992

Family picnic fun at Meyrick Park, for Bolero in the Park, July 1992

The first of the three Bolero in the Park concerts took place with the Bournemouth Symphony Orchestra playing in Meyrick Park, July 1992

BSO musicians survey the crowd before one of the Summer Nights Classics at Upton House, August 1992

Andrew Litton addresses the audience at the BSO Summer Nights Classics at Upton House, August 1992

Top right: BSO's 100 years was celebrated with a centenary concert and special dinner, and a cake. Left to right guest of honour Lord Montagu of Beaulieu, the Lady Digby (President of Bournemouth Orchestras' Council of Management), Principal Conductor Andrew Litton, Nigel Beale, Chairman of Bournemouth Orchestras and Anthony Woodcock, Managing Director, May 1993

Right: Another celebration as violinist Jayne Vickers and Andrew Litton got married in June 1993. They met when Andrew took over at the BSO as Prinicipal Conductor

Composer Sir Michael Tippett, whose work had been performed by the BSO, gave a masterclass at Twynham School, Christchurch, December 1993

Celebrating 100 years of the Bournemouth Symphony Orchestra, a train was given their name at a ceremony at Waterloo Station – exactly 100 years after their very first performance. The BSO and Symphony Chorus were en-route to the Royal Albert Hall for an anniversary concert featuring Mahler's *Resurrection Symphony*. The Orchestra also received a replica of the train nameplate

Andrew Litton, Principal Conductor of the Bournemouth Symphony Orchestra, unveils the train nameplate, May 1993

Luciano Pavarotti rehearsing at Wembley Arena, with conductor Gustav Kuhn, the Bournemouth Symphony Orchestra and the 700 member World Festival Choir, March 1994

Luciano Pavarotti deep in concentration during a rehearsal at Wembley Arena in 1994 for the performance of Verdi's *Requiem*, March 1994

Left: Nigel Beale, left and Tony Woodcock toast the Bournemouth Symphony Orchestra after they scooped the 'Best Large Ensemble' award in the prestigious Royal Philharmonic Music Awards, May 1994

Bottom left: Sir Malcolm Arnold at the piano in the lounge of Bournemouth's Norfolk Royale Hotel. The 73-year-old was in town for a major performance by the Bournemouth Symphony Orchestra of his *Second Symphony* at the Winter Gardens, August 1994

Below: Farewell to Andrew Litton after six years with the BSO. After his final concert at the Winter Gardens Andrew and his violinist wife Jayne were presented with a hand crafted seal during a civic reception at the Russell-Cotes Museum, July 1994

Bournemouth Symphony Orchestra's 100th birthday celebrations. Actor Tom Conti, a lifelong BSO fan, was Master of Ceremonies and fulfilled a childhood ambition to conduct the Orchestra

Former Prime Minister Sir Edward Heath, at rehearsals for the Bournemouth Symphony Orchestra fundraising gala at the Winter Gardens, December 1994

Top left: Yakov Kreizberg Principal Conductor of the BSO

Above: Kevin Field 'conducts' soldier Chris Guy and Terry Nettles as the devil. Strange goings-on during the photocall for forthcoming dramatic roles in Stravinsky's *The Soldier's Tale* at Poole Arts Centre, February 1995

Left: Musicians Celia Craig, Susan Henderson and Terry Nettle on returning from their concert tour, November 1996

Raindrops keep falling on my head... The brollies go up but the crowd is going nowhere at the BSO's Proms in the Park, 2 August 1996 (main image)

Yakov Kreizberg Principal Conductor of the Bournemouth Symphony Orchestra pours energy into the performance, pictured in 1995

Top left: Yakov Kreizberg and the BSO were a big hit in New York's Carnegie Hall, 17 April 1997

Top right: The BSO's Indiana 'Trom' Bones – aka BSO Head of PR Stewart Collins – promoting their Symphonic Soundtracks performance at the BIC, March 1997

Left & bottom left: The BSO's Last Night of the Proms at the BIC, March 1998

The audience gets in the swing of things at the BSO's Last Night of the BSO Proms at the Bournemouth International Centre, March 1998 (bottom right)

Last Night of the BSO Proms at the BIC, March 1998

BSO with Principal Conductor Marin Alsop

2000 to 2008
The new millennium

The beginning of the new millennium promised new things and great excitement for the BSO.

In 2001 the Orchestra once again looked stateside for a principal conductor and announced that from 2002, it would be Marin Alsop, ranked as one of the best young conductors in the world.

She was the first woman to be Principal Conductor of a British Orchestra.

"I am excited and inspired," she said. "I also feel obligated to try to help the next generation of women and young conductors because it is such a difficult area to succeed in."

Alsop, a New Yorker, studied with her childhood mentor, Leonard Bernstein.

She was key to the Orchestra's continued development at home and abroad.

2001 also saw the BSO join the Bach Choir for a gala concert at the Royal Opera House with HRH the Prince of Wales among the guests.

The same year saw a six day residency in Hong Kong with the Orchestra playing under Barry Wordsworth and Lu Jia.

The final concert in the Winter Gardens took place on 20 January 2002.

Its owners, Bournemouth Borough Council, had decided the venue had no long term future. It was soon to be closed and then demolished, despite a big public campaign to save it.

Marin Alsop opened her first season as Principal Conductor. A new BBC Radio 3 partnership ensured regular broadcasts of BSO concerts. This began with Bernstein and Mahler's *Sixth Symphony*.

The same month a performance of *Les Misérables* sold out at the Bournemouth International Centre and it was to be the last Ron Goodwin concert that year, in Poole on 22 December.

The much loved composer and conductor had had a long and hugely popular association with the BSO for nearly 30 years.

But he passed away in January 2003 and the BSO lost a great friend. His music and memory live on.

The BSO's first UK tour under Marin Alsop began in 2003, which also saw the BSO's appearance at the BBC Proms under Alsop.

The outdoor summer concerts that year at various locations proved to be the most popular series so far. Around 40,000 people attended for music, picnics and a great evening outdoors.

The following year that number rose to around 65,000 at venues such as Powderham Castle, Broadlands, Osborne House on the Isle of Wight, Upton Country Park in Poole and Meyrick Park, Bournemouth.

These events showed that classical music could become accessible to much larger numbers than just the traditional concert-going audience.

They have become something of an institution.

And in the years that these huge undertakings

(Continued overleaf)

(Continued overleaf)

In association with

bournemouth
symphony orchestra
BSOlive.com

Marin Alsop, the Bournemouth Symphony Orchestra's Principal Conductor from 2002 to 2008

Below: An accomplished performer on the spoons, conductor Ron Goodwin takes time out for a little practice with BSO trumpeter Barry Latchem, a member of the Orchestra who was on the platform when Ron gave his first Christmas Concert at the Winter Gardens in December 1971

had not been staged, there had been one question. When are they coming back?

Her Majesty the Queen and Prince Philip dropped in at the Lighthouse in July 2004 to watch rehearsals of *Les Misérables*.

The outdoor concerts continued to be a phenomenal success across the south and the BSO, which has the largest touring region of any Orchestra, extended and developed its valuable community work, particularly with schools.

The BSO performed two concerts at the Prague Music Festival in 2005 and that summer the concerts (including two Daily Echo-backed events in Meyrick Park with lasers, lights and fireworks) attracted record ticket sales.

That year Marin Alsop renewed her contract to run until 2008.

The new season opened with a stunning broadcast performance of Mahler's *Resurrection Symphony*, receiving national acclaim.

There were many highlights in 2006.

The annual BSO Benevolent Fund concert was a

tribute to Ron Goodwin, with music ranging from *Where Eagles Dare* to *633 Squadron*.

The BSO was reunited with Yakov Kreizberg at Lighthouse and there were tributes to Abba in Meyrick Park and Sir Malcolm Arnold at Weymouth Pavilion.

Marin Alsop was honoured with a European Woman of Achievement Award in 2007.

As she came towards the end of her tenure she revealed she was a bit of a tearaway as a youngster. "I was a bit of a troublemaker. Then I started taking violin lessons."

Her admission came at the launch of a national initiative to give every one of the country's schoolchildren free entry to a classical music concert. It was another summer of spectacular outdoor events, including the hits of Queen.

At the beginning of 2008, internationally renowned conductor Yan Pascal Tortelier conducted the annual BSO Benevolent Fund concert.

And it would soon be time for a new face as Principal Conductor.

Ron Goodwin and the BSO taken in the Winter Gardens on the occasion of his 75th birthday concert in 2000 (right)

Ron Goodwin recorded internationally and had gold and platinum discs awarded for his film music recordings by EMI

Top left: BSO members' group travel to Hong Kong for the Orchestra's six-day residency. Playing under Lü Jia and Barry Wordsworth they were received with much enthusiasm, August 2001

Above and right: BSO in concert with an Olympic theme, November 2000

Top right: A patriotic note at a BSO open-air concert

Pastoral notes: The Orchestra playing 'al fresco' at Beaulieu, in 2000

BSO members take in the sights of Hong Kong while on tour, August 2001

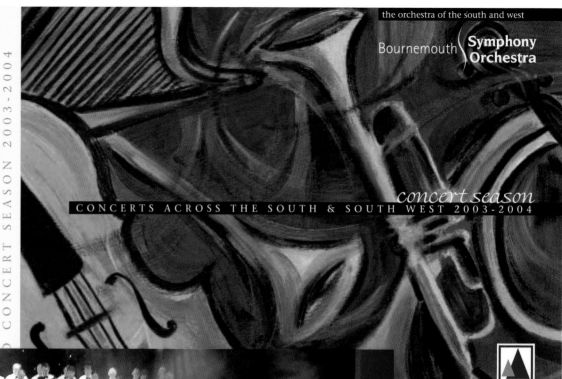

the orchestra of the south and west

Bournemouth Symphony Orchestra

concert season

CONCERTS ACROSS THE SOUTH & SOUTH WEST 2003-2004

CONCERT SEASON 2003-2004

PORTMAN
PRINCIPAL SPONSOR

The sold out BSO concert performance of *Les Misérables* at the Bournemouth International Centre in October 2002

Top left: The Orchestra rehearsing *One Enchanted Evening* with Conductor Pete Harrison, West End stars Earl Carpenter, Spencer McLaren, Anita Louise Combe and Josephina Gabrielle at the Lighthouse, Poole, October 2005

Top right: Local artist Julie Herring was specially commissioned by the BSO to produce this piece of art for the cover of the 2003/2004 brochure

Marin Alsop conducting Shostakovich's *Symphony No.5* at Lighthouse, 24 January 2004

Bottom right: Conductor and composer Martin Yates directing the Bournemouth Symphony Orchestra during the annual concert at Wilton House in 2005

Some of the 7,000 strong audience at the Classical Fireworks Extravaganza featuring the Bournemouth Symphony Orchestra at Wilton House, July 2005 (main and top images)

The spectacular laser and fireworks "Son et Lumière" during the Classical Fireworks Extravaganza featuring the Bournemouth Symphony Orchestra at Wilton House, July 2005

Stunning dancers capture the dramatic mood at the *Live and Let Die* BSO concert in Meyrick Park, August 2005

Thousands of BSO fans gather with their picnics to listen to their favourite Bond themes, August 2005

Top left: Bournemouth Symphony Orchestra present Voulez Vous - The Best of Abba at Meyrick Park... Pictured are Abba Mania (left to right) Paul Curtis, Sharon Wright, Lisa and Martin Curtis, from Parkstone

Bottom left: Abba Performers Paul Robinson, Rebecca Thornhill, Louise Davidson and Kenneth Avery Clarke

Below: The crowd enjoying the BSO's Abba tribute concert

Meyrick Park, Bournemouth full of fans at the BSO Best of Abba concert, August 2006

Flags flying, Bournemouth Symphony Orchestra during rehearsals for the Last Night of the BSO Proms at Colston Hall, Bristol, March 2006

Top left: The crowds enjoy the Bournemouth Symphony Orchestra's Symphonic Queen Spectacular, in Meyrick Park, August 2007

Top and bottom left: The BSO and Bournemouth Symphony Chorus on stage performing the dramatic *Carmina Burana* at Broadlands, August 2007

Russian conductor Tugan Sokhiev leading the BSO, April 2007 (main image)

Bournemouth Symphony Orchestra at Wilton House, July 2007

Top centre: Karabits and the BSO's iconic recording of Tchaikovsky and Mussorgsky

Top right: Heroes and Aliens, Epic Galactic Soundtracks concerts at Lighthouse Poole, Brighton Dome, Guildhall Portsmouth, Colston Hall Bristol and the Great Hall Exeter, February 2016

Bottom right: BSO concert programme for the 2014/15 season

BBC Proms at the Royal Albert Hall, Kirill Karabits and the BSO perform, Britten, Korngold and Prokofiev, August 2015 (main image)

2008 to 2016
Towards 125 years

In 2008 the conductor's baton was laid down by one global star and picked up by another. From west to east.

Marin Alsop departed the BSO and the "energising presence" of Ukrainian-born Kirill Karabits arrived. Karabits, the son of a conductor and composer, made his first public conducting appearance at the age of 19, having studied in Kiev.

He was assistant conductor of the Budapest Festival Orchestra from 1998-2000. From 2002 to 2005 he was principal guest conductor of the Orchestre Philharmonique de Strasbourg.

In November 2007, the BSO announced his appointment as its 13th Principal Conductor after a unanimous vote by the musicians.

He was already known to the BSO having appeared with the Orchestra in 2006 and 2007, both concerts receiving considerable acclaim.

He would take up the post in the 2009-10 season. For 2008-2009 Karabits held the title of Principal Conductor-Designate.

Once again, an inspired choice of conductor had enabled the BSO to reinforce and develop its national and international reputation.

Karabits led the Orchestra on a tour to Germany and also appeared with them three times at the BBC Proms.

2014 saw the release of the first recording of the BSO Prokofiev Symphony cycle.

The recording was described as an outstanding achievement and the Sunday Times noted: "The rich, dark 'Russian' sound and nimble virtuosity he gets are vivid successes of his time in Bournemouth."

In recognition of his work, Karabits was named the Royal Philharmonic Society's Conductor of the Year in May 2013.

The same year the BSO celebrated 120 years with a concert at the Lighthouse, the BBC Proms and two open air performances at the Waterfront in Bournemouth.

"One of my strategic goals was always to play more concerts in Bournemouth because there is nothing stronger than the bond between the orchestra and the city that bears its name," Karabits told the Daily Echo that year.

"We need to involve ourselves more in the life of Bournemouth and establish stronger links with the community."

Speaking of his first visit to Bournemouth he said: "I was invited to come and do Tchaikovsky's *Sixth Symphony* when I was in Strasbourg. I took the train after flying into Heathrow and I got off at Bournemouth station because I did not realise the Orchestra was based in Poole.

(Continued overleaf)

In association with

bournemouth symphony orchestra
BSOLIVE.COM

Kirill Karabits, Chief Conductor of the BSO from 2008 to present day

"I had to get a taxi. It was a bit of a surprise to me. It was my first time to the UK too. I had never been here before.

"I was going to conduct this particular symphony which I knew backwards and I thought it was just another guest conducting so I would do the best I could. Then at the first rehearsal something happened.

"Sometimes it is called chemistry between a conductor and an orchestra, it's difficult to explain. "It's like you meet someone and after five minutes you feel close to them. This happened between me and the BSO. I felt so understood and so happy with them. I always feel that with every performance, they are on the edge. I am proud of what we have achieved together."

The past eight years have seen the BSO's community role grow with schools, hospitals and a multitude of other groups across the region, through its community and education programme, BSO Participate.

These wide ranging initiatives include Tea Dances for senior citizens, Family Orchestra sessions, visiting care homes and pioneering work with dementia patients.

This part of the BSO's remit gives a clue as to its identity. It is the only UK symphony orchestra not based in a major city.

It is a charity, a community organisation, the largest performing arts body in the south and south west and a cultural beacon. It is also a business and a brand.

What happens on stage is only a part of it. Its mission is to deliver the highest quality music and community engagement across a region of 10,000 square miles.

The 2015/2016 season was another huge success. It opened with an outstanding concert staging of Richard Strauss' *Salome*.

Reaction was ecstatic with one national reviewer describing the BSO as "one of this country's cultural miracles." The season also featured a Lighthouse concert to mark the 150th anniversary of the birth of Sibelius.

The new BSO Artist-in-Residence, violinist Augustin Hadelich appeared multiple times across the BSO season and started his journey with Tchaikovsky's Violin Concerto, a perennial favourite of violinists and audiences.

He was later joined by the previous year's Artist-in-Residence Sunwook Kim for a special chamber recital of Mendelssohn's glorious *Octet*.

Violinist Nicola Benedetti released her latest album Shostakovich/Glazunov under the baton of Karabits and the BSO.

The season culminated in the long awaited return of the Proms in the Park in August after a five year absence.

The three day festival in Meyrick Park, backed by the business community and underwritten by Bournemouth Borough Council, saw thousands of music lovers revel in a Classical Extravaganza conducted by the departing Young Conductor in Association, Frank Zielhorst, and Symphonic Abba, with Pete Harrison the following night.

"It's brilliant to be back," the Orchestra's chief executive, Dougie Scarfe, told the audience on the opening night.

The Orchestra is playing incredibly well.

It is, says Scarfe, "in a really great place. People who have watched us for decades are saying how fantastic things are."

Karabits' rolling contract with the BSO has extended his tenure to a minimum date of 2018, fittingly the Orchestra's 125th anniversary. It will be some celebration.

The Bournemouth Symphony Orchestra has indeed gone 'From 1893 to the World.'

Ukrainian conductor Kirill Karabits who won the conductor category at the prestigious Royal Philharmonic Society Awards in 2013

Renowned violinist Nicola Benedetti with the BSO conducted by Kirill Karabits performing Tchaikovsky, Korngold and Prokofiev at the National Concert Hall, Dublin, March 2014

Above: Matthew Wood conducts the Bournemouth Symphony Orchestra Proms in the Park concert at Wilton House, July 2008

Top centre: The audience enthralled at Wilton House, July 2008

A spectacular fireworks display accompanied Tchaikovsky's *1812 Overture* at Wilton House, July 2008

The Bournemouth Symphony Orchestra teamed up with legendary club DJ Danny Rampling for Club K at the Bournemouth International Centre, February 2010

Top left and centre: And the band – and orchestra – played on... at Cunard's Queen Elizabeth cruise liner naming ceremony, October 2010

Below: Getting their groove on, the BSO's violin section at the Symphony Disco Spectacular, Broadlands, August 2011

The BSO play a unique Inside Outdoor Festival at the Lighthouse, conducted by Matthew Wood and accompanied by the Bournemouth Symphony Chorus, June 2010 (bottom left)

Taking a bow: Conductor Pete Harrison and singers, Symphonic Disco Spectacular, Broadlands, August 2011

Right: Martin Grubinger, in rehearsals with the BSO and Kirill Karabits at Lighthouse, Poole, October 2012

Far right: Dougie Scarfe who joined the Bournemouth Symphony Orchestra as Chief Executive, July 2012

Conductor Kirill Karabits leading the Orchestra, July 2013 (above)

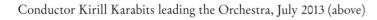

The BSO's Classical Extravaganza with Young Conductor Maxime Tortelier at Portsmouth Guildhall; another popular triumph for the BSO in its 120th anniversary year, July 2013

Left: Dougie Scarfe addresses the audience at the BSO concert at the Pier Approach, August 2014

Top left: Young Conductor in Association, Maxime Tortelier conducts the BSO at the Pier Approach stage, August 2014

Bottom left: Bournemouth Symphony Orchestra, Classical Extravaganza, celebrates the best of classical music, combining a rainbow of symphonic colour with an explosive spectacle of indoor fireworks, lasers and choreographed lighting, June 2014

A special gala concert at the Bournemouth Pavilion to celebrate the 120th anniversary of the BSO, conducted by Kirill Karabits with soloist violinist Nicola Benedetti, May 2013 (top right)

Kirill Karabits and the members of the Bournemouth Symphony Orchestra on the steps of Portsmouth Guildhall, May 2013

The BSO perform Strauss, Prokofiev and Mozart at Colston Hall, Bristol, September 2014

BBC Proms at the Royal Albert Hall, Kirill Karabits and the BSO perform Britten, Korngold and Prokofiev, August 2015

The BSO and Chorus perform at the Classic FM Live concert in the Royal Albert Hall, April 2015

BSO Participate which delivers community engagement programmes across the region 2013-2016

Inspiring young string players, the BSO Blast Strings Project in Gloucestershire, February 2106

2008 to 2016

Top left: Kirill Karabits and the BSO caused a sensation with the performance of *Salome* at Lighthouse, Poole, September 2015

Top right: Frank Zielhorst conducts the Bournemouth Symphony Orchestra through the Classical Extravaganza at Colston Hall, Bristol, July 2015

The BSO perform Richard Strauss' ground-breaking *Salome*, which opened the 2015/2016 season at the Lighthouse, September 2015

Sibelius 150 performed by the BSO with Conductor Kirill Karabits at Lighthouse, Poole, December 2015

Spectacular laser and fireworks displays on the first night of the BSO Proms in the Park, Meyrick Park, Bournemouth, August 2016

Young Conductor in Association, Frank Zielhorst, conducts the BSO Classical Extravaganza, Proms in the Park, August 2016

Top left: Bass players Nicole Boyesen and Nickie Dixon get into the Abba groove

Top centre: Conductor Pete Harrison sets the scene for a fabulous night at Meyrick Park

Top right: Super Trouper BSO and Abba fans

Opposite top left: Singers Dean Collinson, Annie Skates, Emma Kershaw and David Combes nail the Abba hits

Opposite top right: All dressed up, Tom Beer on viola

Pete Harrison conducts the Abba Symphonic Spectacular, Proms in the Park, Meyrick Park, Bournemouth, August 2016

The key players...

Editor and writer: Andy Martin

Photographic selection, research and editing: Michelle Luther

Design and page layout: John Nesbitt, James Barham

Additional research: Tara Russell

Photographic credits: Sussie Ahlburg, Harry Ashley, Jon Beal, John Beasley, Anthony Brown, Paul Carter, Chris Christodoulou, Kevin Clifford, Paul Collins, Stuart Collins, Samantha Cook, Chris Cooper, Ray Cranbourne, Richard Crease, Peter W. Dickenson, Steve Dunlop, John Gilbride, Nicholas Gossip, Stephen Greaves, Tom Gregory, Sasha Gusov, Noel Hardwick, Jo Harvell, Ken Hoskins, Ian Jackson, Richard Johnson, Alwyn Ladell Collection, Christian Lawson, Duncan Lee, Corin Messer, Hattie Miles, Eric Richmond, Andy Scaysbrook, Seeker Photography, Alex Segrave, Christopher Seaman, Sam Sheldon, David Smith, Jonathan Taylor, Pat Timmons, Peter's Collection, The Press Association, Chris Zuidyk

Special thanks to... Barry Meehan, Senior Librarian, Bournemouth Library and volunteer Howard Dalton for all their help with the BSO photographic archives. Also to Dougie Scarfe and Anthony Brown and all the staff at the Bournemouth Symphony Orchestra for their help

Published by:

DAILY ECHO

bournemouthecho.co.uk

In association with

bournemouth
symphony orchestra
BSOlive.com

Newsquest Media (Southern) Ltd,
Richmond Hill,
Bournemouth BH2 6HH

Copyright: Newsquest Media (Southern) Ltd

First published in 2016

ISBN: 978-0-9933533-7-6